Guiding the Single-Staff Church

Guiding the Single-Staff Church

D. G. McCoury,
Author and Compiler

Convention Press • Nashville, Tennessee

This book is the text for course number 23044 in the
subject area
Pastoral Ministries for the Church Study Course
Dewey Decimal Classification: 253
Subject Heading: PASTORAL WORK // CHURCH
ADMINISTRATION
Printed in the United States of America
Available from Baptist Book Stores
Church Administration Department
Sunday School Board, SBC
127 Ninth Avenue, North
Nashville, TN 37234

◆ CONTENTS ◆

◆ **CHAPTER 1** ◆

How and Where to Guide the Single-Staff Church

D. G. McCoury

D. G. McCoury is consultant for pastoral ministries, single-staff church, and the associational program of Pastoral Ministries, Church Administration Department, Baptist Sunday School Board.

The chairperson of the missions development council made an observation about the pastor: "The council is wanting to make plans for starting a new work in the southeast suburb of our city. All members of the council are involved in the give-and-take of our work, but the pastor just attends the meetings. He says nothing—for or against our efforts. We really don't know how he feels about the mission effort, or what his ideas are. As the chairperson, I feel frustrated not knowing where the pastor stands. We all need his input and support." This chairperson felt frustrated with the pastor's *laissez-faire* style of leadership.

The pastor of a young church decided the church treasurer wasn't keeping the books the way the pastor felt the books should be kept. Earlier, when the pastor was a student, he had worked as a bookkeeper. Thus, the pastor decided to take away the bookkeeping from the treasurer and do it himself. As a result, the pastor obligated himself for a specific time each week to "keep books." Later, the treasurer said: "I thought I was doing a good job. If the pastor felt the financial report should follow a certain style, all he needed to do was show me what he wanted." This former church treasurer was frustrated because the pastor used a "take charge" leadership style.

Another pastor used a style of leadership in which he "told" the church what to do. The pastor, wanting to possess power, would share his plans for the church through sermons. When preaching, the pastor said often, "God wants us to _____." A group of concerned church members confronted the pastor about his tactics. The pastor defended his approach by telling the group that because of his spirituality, he knew better than the church as a whole knew what God wanted. That statement made, a dedicated church member shook a finger in the pastor's face and said, "I am just as spiritual as you are!" This church member felt frustrated because he wanted to be heard. He wanted to share his convictions.

These three situations I actually observed during the fifteen years I served as a denominational worker in the Northern Plains Baptist Convention and the Colorado Baptist General Convention. These situations focus on the issue of pastoral leadership in the single-staff church.

In the first illustration, the pastor was not willing to assume the role of leader. In the second, the pastor chose to do something himself rather than to equip or delegate. In the last illustration, the pastor's leadership style was marked by an unhealthy need for control or power.

The three illustrations show ineffective or improper leadership in the given circumstances. In these situations, such continued leadership could result in frustration, confusion, anger, conflict, resignation, or even forced termination. Most important, these examples do not fulfill biblical expectations of responsible leadership.

Leadership styles are important. The type of leadership style modeled by a pastor demonstrates the pastor's values.

Ethical Leadership
Any church will benefit from pastors and volunteer leaders who demonstrate commitment to the church's mission. All churches need leaders who combine biblical principles with effective leadership skills. A Christian leader must be an ethical leader. Are you thinking, *What is an ethical leader?*

Ethical leaders express commitment to a mission. Such leaders are guided by conscience . . . the leadership of the Holy Spirit. For these leaders, values and ideals are twin pillars. Ethical leaders derive pleasure from seeing the church make progress and from enabling other church members to contribute to the church's mission.

The ethical church leader expresses care for individuals. He sees people and their needs as more important than organizational charts. Ethical leaders have a broad perspective of what community means. They care more about relationships than they care about authority and power. They hold up the relational nature of the body of Christ, the church. They believe bad means cannot result in good ends. Ethical leaders know they must earn the trust of their followers. Ethical leaders have integrity—they are guided by Christian conduct and biblical values.

What do these statements mean for leaders in today's single-staff churches? An ethical style of leadership gives integrity to a single-staff pastor. Who the pastor is as a Christian person becomes obvious with the passing of time. The pastor's ethical style of leadership helps him build a base of dependability, trustworthiness, and honesty. These character qualities contribute to the pastor's ability to lead the church.

The goal of Christian leadership is redemption and reconciliation, not winning at any price. Christians are to be prophetic when necessary. This stance requires courage. Christians also must be priestly when necessary. This stance requires love. Above all, God's people must be honest in their purpose. Pastoral ministers must lead without any hint of manipulation.

The single-staff pastor must be, first, an ethical leader, a dependable person of high character, who will not compromise his standards. But, the ethical leader does know the difference between his convictions and his opinions. Convictions are worth contending for. Opinions are not.

Servant Leadership
Is leadership effective when goals have been achieved? when ser-

vice is rendered? one of these? both of these? In the church, we must be careful to hold up servanthood. After all, Jesus' style of leadership was marked by servanthood. Worldly philosophies of "what is in it for me" or "get all you can get" permeate the thinking of some Christians.

Jesus taught that success in Christian living comes from service, not from lording one's position or power over others. Servant leadership shows concern for the well-being of other persons.

Servanthood is the outgrowth of one's profound, transforming experience with Jesus Christ. He is the basis for our faith, our testimony, our integrity. He is our model because of the calling we received in His invitation, "Follow me!"

Team Leadership

Leadership is effective when both the style of leadership and the end results of leadership are compatible. This statement can be illustrated by a quote from Ted Engstrom. "Excellence in leadership requires meaningful relationships with people. [The leader] cannot be an isolated island if he is to be successful. [He] must be armed with every means at his disposal to facilitate the interpersonal growth of an organization. This means he must be quick to learn as much as possible about human nature. Results cannot be forced out of people. They occur only when individuals collaborate under a leader's stimulation and inspiration in striving toward a worthy common goal."[1]

A pastoral ministries leader provides excellent leadership through healthy relationships with other people. The most powerful force shaping the pastor's destiny could be the numbers of persons he involves in the church's ministry. Effective leaders work with and through people. The ability to influence the behavior and decisions of others is basic to all types of leadership. Because the church is a spiritual organism, the church needs a leader who understands and practices teamwork.

Directional Leadership

Single-staff churches differ from multiple-staff churches in geography, size, culture, resources, membership, and church and community needs. Whether the single-staff church is located at a rural crossroads or an urban intersection, the pastor must assume his leadership responsibility if the church fulfills its mission. The single-staff church might be a new-work church or an established church with a two-hundred-year-old heritage. In either case, the church needs a strong, but effective, pastoral leader.

When is a pastor an effective leader? I believe he is effective when he possesses a *clarity of purpose* which fits with *the church's identity.* Clarity of purpose refers to the pastor's sense of mission. The church's identity refers to its history. From a sense of mission grows a vision. And from the church's history grows practical ministries. The church's mission statement becomes the guiding star that gives direction to the church's ministry and programs. If the church doesn't know where it is going, it probably will end up where it doesn't want to be. Knowing what the church is, what its mission is, and what the church wants to accomplish are only three of the qualities which make for effective leadership.

How can a single-staff pastor provide this kind of directional leadership?

• First, he must know the mission of a New Testament church includes worship, proclamation and witness, nurture and education, and ministry.

• Second, the single-staff pastor guides the church to discover ministry needs in the church's community.

• Third, the pastor understands what makes his church unique. By this statement I mean the pastor understands the church's personality.

• Fourth, the pastor helps the church to establish priority needs and to set goals to meet those needs.

In summary, we could say that to guide the single-staff church, a pastoral leader must have (1) integrity of personhood, (2) a commitment to God's call, (3) a sense of purpose, and (4) a leadership style that results in teamwork.

Flexible Leadership

Persons who write about the various kinds of leadership styles often use terms such as passive leader, hermit, dictator, player-coach, people-pleaser, or body leader. But an effective leader isn't one who uses only one style of leadership all the time. An effective leader is a flexible leader. That is, he uses a style of leadership that fits the situation. The circumstances, needs of people, the situation, group maturity level are only four examples of the need to use a flexible style of leadership.

No one leadership style is always the "best" style. Though each pastor will have his own unique style of leadership, he can learn to use other styles. Learning to match the appropriate leadership style with the given situation is one of the keys to becoming a more effective pastoral leader.

Flexibility Illustrated

Four basic leadership styles are available to the pastoral leader. I will give the term that describes that leadership style and a corresponding verb that matches the style: (1) authoritative (telling), (2) consultative (selling), (3) facilitative (participating), and (4) delegative (delegating).

The *authoritative* style reflects a leader who knows what he wants, seems to know how to get what he wants, and is precise, indepenent, and initiating. The *consultative* leader is optimistic, extroverted, friendly, lifts up high standards, and is a good motivator. The *facilitative* style of leader demonstrates a high trust level in people, is willing to share leadership, knows how to be a team member, integrates persons and tasks, and usually is a good developer. The *delegative* style describes a leader who is able to work through people, affirms them, supports them, encourages them, is a player-coach, and lets people have the freedom to be and do. These four leadership styles provide a pastor options for flexibility . . . the ability to use a leadership style that is appropriate to the situation or circumstances.

One way of illustrating how these styles can be used is by describing the role of parents. The first leadership style, authoritative, is the style parents use with a preschool child. Parents have to repeat important facts to the preschooler. For example, "Do not touch! The stove is hot!" The parent assumes a "telling" style of parenting. The authoritative leadership style is often used in a teaching situation. The teacher becomes the authority for the pupil/learner.

The parent of an older child moves more toward a consultative style. In this example, the older child knows the stove is hot. So, the parent encourages the child to act on his knowledge and to begin to take responsibility for his (the child's) actions. Many sermons I hear in Baptist pulpits are of this nature—seeking to get church members to do that which they know they should be doing. Inspiration, or motivation, is a tool effective leaders use. Often a teacher uses group dynamics and lab experiences to get "hands on" involvement as a means of influencing and accommodating learning.

When the child becomes a teenager, the parents move to a facilitative role where collaboration takes place. This style is a participating style. Teenagers are able to do things with you, work in decision making, and set goals for their lives. The parent involves the teen in responsibilities in the home and enjoys friendship with the teen. Assistance, support, and affirmation play a major role in this style of leadership. Teenagers need this kind of guidance.

Once the teenager becomes a young adult, delegation is essential. Maturation has taken place. The apron strings have been cut. The child assumes responsibility for his actions. The parent no longer gives specific directions as an authority figure, but affirms, supports, and encourages the young adult. In each of these examples, if the parent was confused about the needs of each child and used the wrong parenting style, frustration, anger, and anxiety would result.

This same concept speaks to how a leader provides effective leadership. The maturity level, or ability and willingness, of the person or group, becomes the deciding factor for choosing a particular leadership style.

Strengths of Each Style
Each of these four basic leadership styles has specific strengths.

Authoritative	Consultative	Facilitative	Delegative
explains	influences	adapts	develops
clarifies	motivates	meshes	invests
directs	arranges	composes	commits
specializes	classifies	cooperates	enables
approves	harmonizes	befriends	recreates
ascertains	unites	encourages	entrusts
asserts	accommodates	supports	empowers
emphasizes	aligns	sustains	passes on
tells	promotes	assists	assigns

I want to point out that all leaders need all these qualities. But my point is that each style of leadership fits certain needs. The pastoral leader must be sensitive to the style needed in a given situation.

Weaknesses of Excessiveness
While all four of these basic leadership styles are useful, any one of them can become inappropriate. Any strength used in excess can become overpowering. For instance, the authoritative style can be carried to such a point that it becomes coercing. A leader who uses this style to excess can become a dictator who dominates persons, enforces policies and regulations, and coerces

people to do what he wants done.

The consultative style of leader can become a manipulator if he uses this style to excess. The manipulator exploits persons, controls them, and contrives situations.

The facilitative style of leader can take on an air of superiority and become a patronizing person. This individual is often seen as condescending, sometimes being presumptuous and often overbearing.

The delegative leader faces the danger of becoming a *laissez-faire* leader who may go so far as to avoid or shirk responsibility, withdraw, desert the team, or evade the leadership role. Such irresponsibility leaves the group without a leader.

Which Style to Use

How do you determine which leadership style to use? One answer might be to ask the question, Am I dealing with preschoolers, chidren, teenagers, or young adults? Put another way, Is this person or group able to do what I am asking them to do? Do they have the necessary knowledge and skills? Is the person or group willing to do the job? Do the people just need to be inspired? Is their motivation level low? Do they have the confidence to get the job done?

With a new Christian, a pastor would use an authoritative style of leadership, giving specific instruction and closely supervising performance. With a trained Sunday School teacher, a pastor and Sunday School director could use a consultative style of leadership, providing encouragement and motivation. In a deacons' meeting or a Church Council meeting, a pastor would need a facilitative style of leadership. Here the pastoral leader shares ideas, assists, and supports the group in making decisions and/or recommendations to the congregation. Once the Church Council members have made their plans, the pastor assumes a delegative style of leadership with each program organization director. He delegates responsibilities to these individuals.

A pastor must be able to stand in the pulpit and say authoritatively, "Thus saith the Lord." But that same pastor must become a team member who works with the Church Council.

The secret here is using the style of leadership that focuses attention on the church, its mission, and the actions church members can take to help the church accomplish its mission.

How one leads is important, too. Gaines Dobbins once said: "The leader is not one set apart, but one who is identified with the church or a group within the church . . . the less attention he calls to himself, the better leader he is. The more credit the group derives for achievement, the more credible is the leader."[2]

In an earlier book in this series, *Understanding the Single-Staff Church,* I identified three basic types of single-staff churches. In the *family-chapel* church, the power to begin or end things usually rests with one or two significant people, usually a patriarch or matriarch (a deacon chairperson, a Sunday School director, a WMU director, a treasurer). This person is a legitimate leader, respected by the congregation. In this type of single-staff church the pastor functions as a family chaplain who performs weddings and funerals, visits church members in the hospital and nursing homes. The pastor really is a caregiver and preacher, and that is about all. The pastor of a family chapel usually finds his best way of guiding the church is by understanding the administration in the church. Depending on the family-chapel congregation, significant influence can be located in an individual or in a family.

A second type of single-staff church, the *collective alliance,* is built around the leadership of the pastor. In this church, the pastor gathers around him groups of persons he can influence (for example, the Sunday School workers, an influential Sunday School class, persons with special needs, the deacons). In this church everything centers around the pastor. Whereas, the pastor of a family chapel can only *understand* the church's administration, the pastor of the collective alliance *is* the administration. Nothing happens in a collective-alliance church without the pastor's influence or presence.

The third type of single-staff church, the *equipped-leader* church, reflects the sharing of leadership. In this type of church, leadership is traded back and forth between the pastor, elected church leaders, and the congregation as the situation demands. This mutual sharing of leadership allows the pastor to use the full range of the four basic styles of leadership according to circumstances and needs. In the equipped-leader church, the pastor works with committees, councils, and elected church leaders. Therefore, the pastor functions as a genuine leader, rather than only as a caregiver or preacher.

A special challenge arises when a single-staff congregation grows beyond an average Sunday School attendance of one-hundred-fifty to two hundred. The number of programs, relationships, and ministry demands increases to the point that the use of the pastor's time reaches the limits of his humanity. Thus, the pastor must function more and more as a facilitator and as a delegator. He must become the builder of a team, a leader of leaders, who equips elected church leaders to perform their tasks. If the pastor is threatened by the involvement of church members as leaders, he will not function well as the pastor of an equipped-leader church. Conflict can escalate in a church where the pastor and church members struggle over the issue of leadership.

The "How to Guide" Issue

In any discussion about pastoral leadership, the question of authority or power usually is raised. This question implies the pastor either has authority and power or he doesn't. Personally, I do not like to use the words *authority* and *power* when discussing pastoral leadership. I feel this way for several reasons.

For one thing, only Christ possesses ultimate authority or power (see Matthew 28:19-20). Second, what power or authority Jesus has delegated, He has delegated to the church, not to a pastor, a deacon, a WMU director, or a patriarch/matriarch in the church.

A misplaced emphasis on authority and power results in:
• church fights and splits,
• forced termination,
• moving one's membership to another church,
• withholding tithes and offerings,
• poor reputation in the community, and
• jockeying for position.

All believers are accountable to God through Christ. All believers are ministers. All believers have been spiritually gifted for ministry. All believers must be guided by the authority of Holy Scripture. All believers should be responsible, Christian witnesses.

What then, is the role of the pastor and other church leaders? They must affirm and equip fellow believers thereby producing a dynamic force of Christians who are led by the Holy Spirit. The pastor of a single-staff church shoulders the responsibility for preparing church members for the work of ministry by involving "the ministers" (church members) in the church's ministry. The pastor, as the God-called and church-affirmed leader, serves the Lord and the congregation by equipping, enabling, and affirming church members for ministry. (See Ephesians 4:11-16.) The pastor who fails in his equipping/enabling/affirming role turns aside God's intention in calling the pastor.

Church members develop a sense of ownership in what the church is doing only when those members have been encouraged to dream for the church. In the democratic form of church government, consensus and cooperation are effective approaches. Even in today's business world, successful companies have moved away from fixed systems to more responsible systems. A domineering style of leadership is not an effective style to use with volunteer workers in the church. Persons who feel they are being treated as pawns tend to be passive toward the leader who gets his satisfaction from dominating those persons. No church member wants to become a pawn to the pastor.

If a pastoral leader wants to have an effective ministry he must encourage his followers to accomplish worthy things on their own. He must encourage the church to dream its own dreams. Then, he equips/enables the church to accomplish those dreams.

After all, it is the congregation as a whole, not just the pastor, who does mission. The church does not "hire" a pastor to do the church's job. Rather the church calls a pastor to equip church members to do their mission.

Biblically and historically the church has taken three specific actions to help itself in doing its mission:

• It has called a pastor.
• It has selected deacons.
• It has elected volunteer leaders.

The church has this leadership team for the purpose of accomplishing its mission. But note: the leadership team of pastor, deacons, and volunteer leaders does not do the church's mission for the church. Rather, this team of leaders enables the congregation in carrying out its mission.

The pastor serves as leader of this team. He understands from God's Word that his role is to equip (task) the people of God (who) to do mission (purpose) for church growth (results). We might illustrate this concept by using the diagram on page 18.

The best way for a pastor to begin an equipping ministry at a church is by first equipping this leadership team of deacons and volunteer leaders (Church Council members, church officers, and church committee members). In this way, the pastor becomes the equipper of the equippers.

The single-staff pastor can't individually equip each member of the church. For example, consider a church of one hundred members. If the pastor organized study and training groups of eight to ten persons, he would have about twelve such groups. And if he

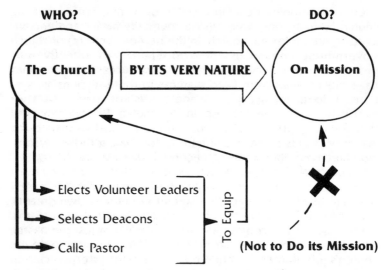

devoted one hour a week to each group, he would have to give at least ten hours a week to this task of equipping the groups. And that doesn't include the time required to prepare for each of these study/training sessions.

A better approach is for the pastor to equip the deacons and volunteer leaders who then, in turn, equip the persons who work with them. Let's consider the Sunday School director as an example. The pastor can provide the instruction and training needed by the Sunday School director so he or she can lead the Sunday School teachers to provide the quality of Bible study that meets the church's needs.

How can a pastor equip a Sunday School director? The pastor shares all he knows about Sunday School work—the purpose and tasks of Sunday School, the organization of the Bible teaching program. The pastor helps the Sunday School director acquire available resources (Church Study Course books, quarterlies, Sunday School leadership periodicals).

When the local association provides training for Sunday School directors, the pastor enlists the Sunday School director to attend these training meetings. At typical associational training meetings, the Sunday School director would be made aware of state convention and SBC resources for effective Sunday School work. The pastor also could enlist the Sunday School director to attend training conferences at state assemblies or at Ridgecrest and

Glorieta Baptist Conference Centers.

Serving as a resource person might be one of the pastor's best strengths as an equipper. The pastor's goal is to enable the Sunday School director to know more about Sunday School work than the pastor knows. After all, the Sunday School director is the church's elected Sunday School specialist!

When a teacher calls the pastor on Sunday morning seeking a substitute for his or her class, the pastor can lovingly direct the teacher to contact the Sunday School director. The pastor never goes around the director in matters related to the church's Sunday School program. The Sunday School director is the pastor's companion in ministry, not the pastor's competitor.

Let's consider another example. In many single-staff churches, the pastor is burdened with weekly hospital and nursing home visitation. This fact is especially true in single-staff churches who expect a "ministry of presence" from their pastor. And if the various hospitals and nursing homes are scattered around the town or city, the demands on the pastor's time are even greater.

The pastor can equip deacons to minister in hospitals and nursing homes. One way the pastor does this is by taking individual deacons with him as he (the pastor) visits the hospitals and nursing homes. The pastor models effective visitation and the deacons learn from the pastor's example. Available, also, are numerous printed deacon resources that can become the basis for deacon training sessions on effective hospital and nursing home visitation (see resource list at the end of Chapter 7).

The "Where" to Guide Issue

"Where" do we guide the church? The answer to this question must be a biblical one because the church is God's agent of redemption in our world. Jesus is lord and head of the church. The church has been Divinely commissioned (see Matthew 28:19-20).

This commission emphasizes church growth. The church is the body of Christ, and bodies are meant to grow. God expects church growth. Church growth is normal. The church must take the initiative to grow.

But in what ways is the church to grow? What kind of church growth is biblical growth?

Balanced Church Growth

Often we focus on only one element of church growth and,

therefore, develop a lopsided church. The leaflet *Growing South-ern Baptist Churches* defined church growth as "the Divine-human process of adding to a church those who are saved through Jesus Christ, equipping them for responsible discipleship resulting in witnessing, ministering, and establishing new fel-lowships of believers."

This definition shows that church growth is a process. The pas-tor who guides a single-staff church to grow will be leading that church in a process of growth, the process of "building up the body of Christ." This growth process includes:

• Evangelism (the outreach issue—numerical growth, witness-ing, reaching those without Christ);

• Discipleship (the personal issue—training, nurturing, de-veloping into mature disciples those who have been reached);

• Missions (the extension issue—establishing new witness points, mission Vacation Bible Schools, mission Sunday Schools, Backyard Bible Clubs, giving to world missions through the Coop-erative Program, doing mission action projects, starting a new church);

• Administration (the functional issue—guiding the church through change, uniting the members into a fellowship and pro-tecting the fellowship, maintaining the organization).

Biblical Support for Balanced Church Growth

Because we look to the Bible as our authority for our faith and practice, let's ask: Is there a biblical basis for these four areas of balanced church growth?

In the first area, *evangelism* (the outreach issue), the result of growth is an increase in the total number of believers/church members. As the Bible records the development of the early church, it reflects a picture of an ever-increasing number of per-sons who were brought to faith in Christ and into the church. The early church was evangelistic in nature, and numerical growth re-sulted from the church's efforts. Several times in the Book of Acts we read of numerical growth (Acts 2:41,47; 4:4; 5:14; 6:7; 11:21).

Discipleship growth (the personal issue) is described in Acts 2:42: "And they continued steadfastly in the apostles' doctrine and fellowship, and in breaking of bread, and in prayers." Paul gave an exhortation for this kind of growth: "As ye have therefore received Christ Jesus the Lord, so walk ye in him: rooted and built up in him, and stablished in the faith, as ye have been taught, abounding therein with thanksgiving" (Col. 2:6-7). Training, nurturing, and equipping were ongoing tasks in the early church. Read also Acts 16:15, 2 Timothy 3:16-17.

The third area, *missions* (the extension issue), results in an increase in the total number of congregations. Paul and other disciples traveled from place to place starting new churches. Paul might be considered as the original church planter. Scriptures providing support for extension growth are: Acts 8:4-17; 11:19-24; 13:1-3; 18:11; and 1 Corinthians 16:8.

Administrative growth (the functional issue), results in the growth of relationships and fellowship in the body of Christ. The result of this kind of growth is that church members are able to work effectively together. Bible verses supporting administrative growth are: Acts 6:1-7; 9:26-31; 11:1-4; 15:1-34; Ephesians 4:15-16; 1 Corinthians 12:12-16; 14:26,40. Charles Tidwell wrote:

> There are certain functional areas in which the administrative leader must function, regardless of the forms of the organizations chosen to implement the action. A functional area of church administration is a part of the field in which leaders perform certain administrative actions which are natural, characteristic, and essential to the life of the organism, the church. These are the functional areas which comprise the field of church administration:
> - purpose
> - objective
> - program (or ministry plan)
> - organization
> - human resources
> - physical resources
> - financial resources
> - control
>
> The common thread which weaves through all the administration functions is that the nature of the functions is leading. Not all administration and leading are synonymous, but all administration is related to leading, if it is good administration . . . The administrator leads and guides persons by performing certain basic skills in the particular functional areas indicated.[3]

Church growth doesn't occur by itself. Churches grow as they are led to grow by the Holy Spirit's work through the commitment and action of leaders. Bruce Grubbs made this point:

> When a pastor would lead the church to grow, he is seeking to influence persons to accept Christ and unite with the church. This is evangelism. When he works to help believers grow in their faith and personhood, he is equipping believers. This is what Jesus

meant when He said to make disciples. As he (the pastor) works to help the Sunday School and Church Training leaders work together toward a common objective or to guide a committee toward a progressive recommendation or action, he is influencing, leading toward growth. This is the development of the body. As the pastor seeks to call forth the interest, energy, and resources of the church to undergird new groups of Christians, he is leading growth. This is missions. The four areas of influencing or leadership form the areas of action for the effective growth leader.[4]

Francis DuBose, missions professor at Golden Gate Baptist Theological Seminary observed: "From every source of understanding behind the reason for growth, one thing always emerges as significant—leadership."[5]

This principle of effective leadership has been identified as the constant factor among churches that are growing. Church growth results from effective leadership.

Pastoral leaders and other elected church leaders must guide their churches to grow in these four areas. What is involved is an intentional ministry that leads the church to be on mission.

To help our understanding of the guiding process, the following chapters in this book will include presentations of various program tasks. The purpose of this approach is to heighten the leader's awareness about the "handles" of various church programs. Each program task mentioned in the following chapters falls under one or more of the four functions of the church: worship, proclaim and witness, nurture and educate, and minister. These functions are the result of the church's intention due to its mission. One way of explaining this point is by using the illustration on pages 25-29.

Because this book presents an overview of the basic programs and their tasks, the reader should realize that I am dealing with the whys more than I am dealing with the hows. My objective is to show why the program tasks help the church perform its mission, and to refer to a few basic resources for each program.

These resources will represent the hows of the individual program. Because this book is an administrative book, there will be more content related to the Pastoral Ministries tasks, those carried out by the pastor, deacons, Church Council members, church officers, and church committee members.

[1]Ted W. Engstrom, *The Making of a Christian Leader* (Grand Rapids: Zondervan, 1976), 194-196, 120.

[2]Gaines S. Dobbins, *A Ministering Church* (Nashville: Convention Press, 1960), 55.

[3]Charles A. Tidwell, *Church Administration: Effective Leadership for Ministry* (Nasville: Broadman Press, 1985), 49-50.

[4]Bruce Grubbs, author-compiler, *Helping a Small Church Grow* (Nashville: Convention Press, 1980), 13-14.

[5]Francis DuBose, *How Churches Grow in an Urban World* (Nashville: Broadman Press, 1978), 169.

Resources

Brown, J. Truman, Jr. *Visionary Leadership for Church Growth. Nashville: Convention Press* (available September 1990).

Church Administration, Church Literature Order Form.

Dale, Robert D. *Ministers as Leaders.* Nashville: Broadman Press, 1984.

Dale, Robert D. *Sharing Ministry with Volunteer Leaders.* Nashville: Convention Press, 1986.

Dobbins, Gaines S. *Learning to Lead.* Nashville: Broadman Press, 1968.

McCoury, D. G. *Understanding the Single-Staff Church.* Nashville: Convention Press, 1988.

Orr, Robert. *Being God's People: a Southern Baptist Church on Bold Mission.* Nashville: Convention Press, 1987.

Powell, Paul W. *The Nuts and Bolts of Church Growth.* Nashville: Broadman Press, 1982.

Powers, Bruce P. *Christian Leadership.* Nashville: Broadman Press, 1979.

Stacker, Joe R. and Bruce Grubbs. *Shared Ministry: a Journey Toward Togetherness.* Nashville: Convention Press, 1985.

Stacker, Joe R. and Bruce Grubbs. *Shared Ministry: Beginning the Journey Toward Shared Ministry.* Nashville: Convention Press,1987.

Stacker, Joe R. and Bruce Grubbs. *Pastoral Leadership Skills for Growing Churches,* Nashville: Convention Press, 1988.

Sullivan, James. *Southern Baptist Polity at Work in a Church.* Nashville: Convention Press, 1988.

Organizing the Work of a Church

MISSION — — —→   FUNCTIONS — —→   PROGRAMS

Purpose Statement	Worship	BASIC PROGRAMS
This states a church's reason for being—the basic purpose for which it exists. *The functions grow out of mission and should lead a church to do its work in ways consistent with its nature and mission.*	Proclaim and Witness Nurture and Educate Minister *Functions are administered through church programs. Each program has tasks that carry out church functions.*	Pastoral Ministries Bible Teaching Church Training Music Ministry Brotherhood Woman's Missionary Union EMPHASIS PROGRAMS Family Ministry Stewardship Evangelism Missions Development Vocational Guidance Student Ministries SERVICE PROGRAMS Media Library Recreation Services Administrative Services

TASKS

All the church tasks are performed by one of the various church programs. Each one of these tasks enables the church to accomplish one or more of its functions.	These tasks are all listed on page 26. These tasks define the continuing activity performed by a church to carry out its functions in accomplishing its mission.

CHURCH FUNCTIONS:
- Worship
- Proclaim and Witness
- Nurture and Educate
- Minister

Basic Church

Basic Church Programs

PASTORAL MINISTRIES

Involved: Pastors, church staff, deacons, Church Council, church officers, and committees.

1. Lead the church in the accomplishment of its mission.

2. Proclaim the gospel to believers and unbelievers.

3. Care for the church's members and other persons in the community.

BIBLE TEACHING

Involved: Sunday School officers and teachers, and V.B.S. workers.

1. Reach persons for Bible study.

2. Teach the Bible.

3. Witness to persons about Christ and lead persons into church membership.

4. Minister to persons in need.

5. Lead members to worship.

CHURCH TRAINING

Involved: Church Training officers and workers.

1. Reach persons for discipleship training.

2. Orient new church members for responsible church membership.

3. Equip church members for discipleship and personal ministry.

4. Teach Christian theology and Baptist doctrine, Christian ethics, Christian history, and church polity and organization.

5. Train church leaders for ministry.

All Programs—Interpret and undergird the work

Programs

Task Statements

MUSIC MINISTRY

Involved: Choir directors, members, and age group leaders.

1. Provide musical experiences in congregational services.

2. Provide church music education.

3. Lead the church to witness and minister through music.

4. Assist church programs in providing training in music skills and in consultation about music equipment.

BROTHERHOOD

Involved: Baptist men, officers and age group leaders, plus men and boys.

1. Engage in missions activities.

2. Teach missions.

3. Pray for and give to missions.

4. Develop personal ministry.

WOMAN'S MISSIONARY

Involved: Baptist women and Baptist young women, officers and age group leaders, plus women and girls.

1. Teach missions.

2. Engage in mission action and personal witnessing.

3. Support missions.

of the church and the denomination.—All Programs

Service Programs*

Media Library
Provide, promote, and train persons in the use of media and media library services.

Recreation Services
Provide recreation methods, materials, services, and experiences that will enrich the lives of persons and support the total mission of the church.

Administrative Services
Assist the church to plan its program, manage its resources, and govern its life and work.

Emphasis Programs**

Family Ministry
Minister to the distinctive needs of couples, parents and their children, senior adults, and single adults.

Stewardship
Develop Christian stewards and support Cooperative Program ministries.

Evangelism
Engage the church to develop a comprehensive church strategy of evangelism, involve church members in personal evangelism, and reach persons for Christ through special events and mass evangelism.

Missions Development
Identify mission needs/opportunities, develop missions strategies to respond to unmet needs, establish new churches, and support establishing and strengthening WMU and Brotherhood.

Vocational Guidance
Educate in Christian vocation and guide persons in church occupation and adjustment.

Student Ministry
Assist in fulfilling the mission of the church by leading students
and others in the academic community to faith in God through
Jesus Christ as Savior and Lord, to guide them in Christian growth
and discipleship, and to involve them in responsible church membership.

*Service programs encompass tasks that support the con-
gregation and the six basic programs in doing their work.
**Emphasis programs are channeled by all appropriate staff, com-
mittees, and/or church programs.

◆ **CHAPTER 2** ◆

Evangelism: Strengthening Outreach

Bill May

Bill May is director, Church Services Division, Arizona Southern Baptist Convention, Phoenix, Arizona.

I met with Bill and Wes for lunch one day to discuss how I could best serve their church, Trinity Baptist Church, as its interim pastor. Bill was a young attorney with a sense of humor and unrestrained enthusiasm for his church. Wes was a young businessperson who projected warmth and compassion when he spoke. Both these men served as deacons and adult Sunday School teachers. Both men had been members of Trinity church for many years. Our conversation focused on the needs of the church and the type of leadership the church needed. Wes described personal needs of members requiring the ministry of a pastor. Bill perceived

the need for a pastor who could help the church identify its mission and then challenge the people to be involved. One word Bill used to describe the pastor was a *catalyst*—someone who would pull the people together and say, "Let's go, folks!"

In the book, *Leading Your Church to Grow,* Peter Wagner stated: "While both the pastor and the people must want their church to grow and be willing to pay the price, the order is significant. With few exceptions, the pastor must be motivated for growth first, and then the people. Only in very rare cases will the people become motivated and then get the pastor excited about growth."[1]

How can the single-staff pastor become a catalyst for evangelistic church growth? That is what this chapter is about.

Make a Commitment to Evangelistic Growth

The commitment of a warmhearted, dedicated pastor always makes the difference in a church's ministry effectiveness. Few churches will become openly evangelistic apart from the dedication and commitment of its pastor.

A smaller membership single-staff church in Florida called a young pastor. He had devoted his life to the ministry and was totally committed to have a major outreach emphasis. He believed every church could and ought to grow. When this pastor began preaching about reaching people and about growing a strong Sunday School, the members quickly informed him there were no prospects in the community. After all, they reasoned, they knew where every person lived and where every person attended church. These church members believed strongly there were no unreached people around them.

The pastor dealt patiently with the people, but he kept on preaching and kept on calling for growth. He worked with the Sunday School workers to reorganize the church's Sunday School organization for growth. He led the church to establish a visitation program. He encouraged church members to join him each week as he visited in the homes of persons in that little community.

At the end of the year, that country church had doubled its Sunday School enrollment and attendance. But, best of all, the church had baptized sixty-five persons. All of that occurred in a community that (supposedly) had no prospects![2]

A pastor takes a bold step toward evangelistic church growth when he makes a commitment to his church's Sunday School.

Why? The answer lies in the tasks of the Sunday School. In other words, the basic things the Sunday School can accomplish will lead the church toward growth.

The single-staff pastor must magnify the mandate of the Great Commission (Matt. 28:19-20). And the church has no better program for accomplishing the Great Commission than the Bible Teaching program (Sunday School).

Magnify the Tasks of Sunday School

The tasks of Sunday School come directly from the mission of the church.

1. *Reach people for Bible study.*—Few people are disciplined enough to do Bible study on their own. This means that if people are to study the Bible, we must enroll them in Sunday School classes. Encourage your Sunday School classes to enroll people in Sunday School. The Bible study people will receive on Sunday morning is not all the Bible study people need. But that time of Bible study on Sunday morning is more than what most people receive. As you encourage planned visitation and regular outreach, you can lift high the importance of enrolling people in Sunday School.

2. *Teach the Bible.*—The Bible, God's holy Word, is alive and relevant for today's issues. Every person needs to study the Bible. Every person can profit from Bible study. Encourage your church's Sunday School teachers to do a good job of Bible teaching. Provide training that will help them improve their Bible teaching skills. And show them how to apply scriptural truths to people's lives.

3. *Witness to persons about Christ and lead them into church membership.*—As people are enrolled in Sunday School, and as the Bible is taught to them, and as they rub shoulders with caring class members, their hearts are prepared for a presentation of the gospel. Urge your Sunday School teachers to be openly evangelistic. Whenever unsaved people are present in Sunday School classes, encourage teachers to find ways to tie the lesson into a presentation of the gospel.

4. *Minister to Sunday School members and nonmembers.*—Sunday School is people. And the people in Sunday School classes have many needs. Some are physically ill. Some are grieving. Others are seeking God's will about important life decisions. Many are confused. Some have problem marriages. All deal with the stressors of daily living. What members of Sunday School

classes need, in addition to Bible study, is care. Train Sunday School workers in caring skills. Do all you can to influence all Sunday School classes to become caring, ministering classes.

5. *Lead members to worship.*—In most churches, a worship service follows Sunday School. Class members should be encouraged to attend congregational worship services. But private worship also is needed. For this reason, Sunday School members can be encouraged to feed daily on God's Word, to cultivate their prayer lives, and to establish personal and family devotions.

6. *Interpret and undergird the work of the church and the denomination.*—The Sunday School is the largest organization in the church and has the most members. Isn't it reasonable, then, that the Sunday School should help interpret the work of the church and the denomination? The Sunday School can provide enthusiastic support for all church activities and programs.

What are the dreams you have for your church's outreach? Be assured that if you will give attention to the Sunday School, this organization can do more to produce evangelistic growth than any other organization in the church.

Manage the Steps Toward Sunday School Growth

The Sunday School has been around for a long time. A man named Robert Raikes is credited for getting the Sunday School movement going. His influence was felt during the late eighteenth century. Since that time, churches that have majored on having the best Sunday School possible, have seen evangelistic growth.

Because Sunday School has been with us for more than two hundred years, certain Sunday School strategies have been proved to yield the greatest fruit. Here are these steps for Sunday School growth. Manage these steps well and you will have not only a growing Sunday School, but also a growing church.[3]

1. *Identify and enroll prospects.*—A prospect is a person who is not involved in the ministry of a church. But a better way of viewing a prospect is to see him or her as a person whom God loves and for whom Jesus died.

Prospects have to be discovered; they don't usually seek a church. A good way to find prospects is by developing a prospect file. This file could be as simple as a stack of cards on which are written the names and other information of persons who are prospects for your church. Every church needs such a file. When you have a prospect file, you can share the names of prospects with the various Sunday School classes. Those classes then have the name of an actual person who needs a visit or contact from that class.

Some churches have benefited from having a welcome desk near the entrance to the church. Persons who serve at the welcome desk greet visitors, assign them to a Sunday School class, and seek to enroll them in the Sunday School.

Make use of Sunday School enrollment cards. These cards could be placed in the hymnal racks in the worship center. Persons not enrolled in Sunday School could be encouraged to fill out an enrollment card and then place the card in the offering plate when it is passed. Then an appropriate Sunday School class could follow up on the person(s) who filled out the enrollment card(s).

Seek to enroll all your new church members in a Sunday School class. Enroll people when you visit in their homes. Enroll children who attend your church's Vacation Bible School. Conduct special enrollment emphases. Schedule times of visitation for the very purpose of discovering prospects and enrolling them in Sunday School.

The secret to effective enrollment procedures is to assign all prospect names to Sunday School classes for future visits and contacts.

2. *Start new Sunday School classes.*—The Sunday School director, working with the church's Sunday School leaders, can enlarge the church's Sunday School by adding additional Sunday School classes. Persons who can teach these new classes must be enlisted and trained.

Sunday School classes function best when class members are grouped by age. In most cases, when adult Sunday School classes reach about twenty-five persons on roll, it is time to begin a new class. In the youth (grades 7-12) area, when enrollment exceeds fifteen youth, new classes are recommended. Children's and preschool classes often need more than one worker. The suggested pupil-teacher ratio in children's departments is 1 to 7; and the suggested ratio in preschool departments is 1 to 4. When these pupil-teacher ratios are exceeded this may be an indication of the need to begin new classes in these departments.

Why begin new classes? Why not allow classes to become as large as possible? One reason is that new classes tend to grow faster. Also, classes that become large often lose their vision for reaching out to new persons. And, large classes sometimes exceed the space they have in which to meet, creating crowded classrooms. Too, new classes allow a church to group Sunday School members more closely with persons their own age.

3. *Enlist and train new workers.*—New classes will require additional workers. Study your church roll. List the names of possible Sunday School workers. Ask two questions of each name: (1) Could this person serve if willing? and (2) Would this person be acceptable to the church?

Another approach that works well in many churches is to use a talent survey. A card for this survey can be obtained from Baptist Book Stores, or you can make one of your own. On the card should be listed the various jobs in the church and a place for the person filling out the survey to check his or her interest in working in that job.

Use the nominating committee. Ask members of this committee to make a personal visit to each person you want to enlist as a worker. Explain the job that is needed and the requirements and expectations of that job. Give the person time to pray about his or her acceptance of the job.

Once new workers have been enlisted they should be trained. New workers can receive training through personal study. Many books about age-level Sunday School work are available. Provide such books for your new workers to study. Present Sunday School workers can give training assistance to new workers. Your association has persons who stand ready to provide training for your church's Sunday School workers. And don't forget that your state convention sponsors training opportunities, too. Sunday School workers, both experienced and inexperienced, can receive training on a national basis at Ridgecrest and Glorieta Baptist Conference Centers.

4. *Provide needed space and equipment.*—If your church is serious about growing an evangelistic Sunday School, the church must provide needed space and equipment. Analyze the space you have available for Sunday School classes. Are there rooms not being used currently that could become Sunday School rooms? Sometimes space has to be reassigned. For example, a class having a large attendance in a small room might swap rooms with a class having a small attendance but located in a large room. Once all existing space has been used, providing new space should be considered.

Remember that classes often protect "their turf!" This is especially true in smaller membership churches, where feelings are more important than efficiency. Classroom changes should be negotiated and worked out with all involved well before the change is made.

Do your teachers and classes have the equipment they need to do a good job of teaching and learning? Do classrooms have adequate numbers of chairs and tables? Do teachers have chalkboards, maps, bulletin boards, easels, and shelves? Teachers in preschool and children's areas need special kinds of equipment—record players and records, books, musical instruments, painting equipment, puzzles, pictures, home living equipment (play stove, play refrigerator, table, chairs, etc.), blocks, and much more.

Yes, this equipment does cost money. But your church's failure to provide this kind of needed equipment could demoralize your Sunday School workers.

5. *Conduct regular workers' meetings.*—Conduct these meetings weekly, bi-monthly, or monthly. These meetings give Sunday School workers an opportunity to do planning together, as a team. In these meetings leaders solve problems, discuss the coming Sunday's lesson, promote attendance and enrollment campaigns, minister to workers, pray for the Sunday School, and encourage disheartened workers.

Regular (preferably weekly) workers' meeting can be held in smaller membership churches. Workers can gather with other workers who teach similar age pupils. Here is a suggested agenda:

• General meeting of all workers to discuss any upcoming plans and to pray;

• Review lesson and Bible passage for the coming Sunday's lesson;

• Discuss the learners' needs;

• Talk about the aim of next Sunday's lesson;

• Determine teaching objectives;

• Decide on possible teaching methods to be used in next Sunday's lesson;

• List needed resources and make assignments;

• Share ideas about applying the lesson to life.

A regular workers' meeting might be a new experience for your church's Sunday School workers. The key to effectiveness with these meetings is to plan well for them. One or two bad, unplanned meetings is all that is needed to bring the end to any future workers' meetings. The Sunday School director should encourage all Sunday School workers to make plans for teaching improvement.

6. *Conduct regular visitation.*—Growing an evangelistic church is hard work, and regular visitation is part of that work. Here are some suggestions for an effective visitation program.

Organize it. You need persons in charge who can keep the prospect file up-to-date and who can make and keep up with visitation assignments.

Schedule it. Place on the church calendar specific times for visitation of Sunday School prospects.

Train the visitors. Teach them the principles for making an effective visit. Teach them to handle problems and objections. Teach them to share their faith with the unsaved.

The pastor must support it. What better way is there for a pastor to work with church members than to visit with them?

Make different kinds of visits. Some visits will need to be made to the unsaved. Christians who are prospects for church membership need a visit. Persons who are going through times of personal difficulties need a visit. Absentees need visits.

Affirm persons who visit. Recognize them publicly. Have these visitors share testimonies of what visitation means to them. Print their names in the Sunday bulletin.

Conduct special visitation events. Don't limit all your visitation efforts to weekly or monthly visitation. Plan and promote special times of intensive visitation for specific purposes, such as a visitation emphasis prior to a revival. Make these times fun and exciting.

7. *Teach the Bible.*—Unsaved persons can be won to Christ through effective Bible teaching. Bible teaching encourages Christians to be better disciples of Christ. Because of the values of Bible study, do all you can to help your Sunday School teachers be the best teachers they can be.

Make Use of Other Evangelistic Events

Your Sunday School will probably be your church's primary evangelistic tool for church growth. But your church can use other evangelistic emphases, too. Here are some suggestions:

1. *Vacation Bible School.*—Many boys and girls can be reached for Christ through a week of Vacation Bible School during the summer. The amount of Bible teaching provided during Vacation Bible School is greater than the amount of Bible teaching that can be provided during several months of Sunday School time.

Conduct an evangelistic service at the end of Vacation Bible School. Offer children who are spiritually ready an opportunity to receive Christ. Be sure to follow-up on each child who makes a decision. For many single-staff churches, Vacation Bible School is the biggest evangelistic event of the year. Use the VBS transfer plan and enroll in your Sunday School classes the names of all boys and girls who attended your VBS who are not connected with some other church. The parents of these children are also prospects for your church.

2. *Backyard Bible Clubs and Mission VBS.*—A Backyard Bible Club is both a recreation and a Bible study event. Your church finds a spot in a neighborhood, advertises the Backyard Bible Club, and then conducts a brief time of Bible study for boys and girls. A recreation and refreshment time is a part of Backyard Bible Club. This kind of event can be an excellent public relations tool for your church. But primarily, this kind of event will help you locate additional prospects.

A Mission Vacation Bible School can be conducted in an area where no other church will conduct a VBS. Perhaps there is an area of your town where a church is needed. Or, maybe there is a pocket of people in your community where no church has a witness. These kinds of locations are excellent for Mission VBS. This kind of outreach might open the door for starting a new church. The Mission VBS materials are designed for boys and girls with limited church experience.

See the resource page at the end of this chapter for information about materials for Vacation Bible School, Mission Vacation Bible School, and Backyard Bible Clubs.

3. *Revivals.*—Churches should have revival meetings for at least four reasons.[4] First, revival meetings reach the unsaved and unchurched. In past years, revivals have produced about half of the professions of faith and baptisms in Southern Baptist churches.

Second, revival meetings reach uninvolved church members. A revival can be an excellent way for a church to reclaim many of its church members who have become inactive.

Third, revival meetings edify Christians. Church members who come to revival services night after night usually make new commitments and experience a new closeness to God.

Fourth, revival meetings strengthen churches. A well-planned, prayed-up revival meeting can result in your church's spiritual renewal. The resource page at the end of this chapter lists resources for planning revival meetings.

4. *Special days.*—Smaller membership churches know the benefits to be gained from celebrating special days in the life of the church—a homecoming, a church anniversary, are two examples. These events can be more than just fun times for the church family. Make them evangelistic. Precede the event with a night of visitation. Plan an evangelistic worship service on the day of the special event.

Pastor, your enthusiasm for evangelism will be contagious. Reaching the lost for Christ is the greatest challenge facing all churches today. Examine your commitment regarding evangelistic growth. Renew your calling. Build a good Sunday School. Plan evangelistic events.

---

[1]C. Peter Wagner, *Leading Your Church to Grow* (Ventura, CA: Regal Books, 1984).

[2]Adapted from *Growing and Winning Through the Sunday School,* Harry M. Piland, comp., (Nashville: Convention Press, 1981), 15.

[3]Material in this section was adapted from *Growing and Winning Through the Sunday School,* Harry M. Piland, comp., (Nashville: Convention Press, 1981).

[4]Bill V. Cathey, *A New Day in Church Revivals,* (Nashville: Broadman Press, 1984), 13-14.

Resources

Cathey, Bill V. *A New Day in Church Revivals.* Nashville: Broadman Press 1984.

Chatham, James W. *How to Discover, Enlist, and Train Sunday School Workers.* Nashville: Convention Press, 1982.

Heath, Daryl. *The Small Sunday School at Work.* Nashville: Convention Press, 1981.

Herring, Jerri. *Finding Sunday School Prospects.* Nashville: Convention Press, 1984.

Piland, Harry M. *Basic Sunday School Work.* Nashville: Convention Press, 1980.

Piland, Harry M., compiler. *Growing and Winning Through the Sunday School.* Nashville: Convention Press, 1981.

Shotwell, Bob Edd. *How to Start and Maintain a Weekly Worker's Meeting.* Nashville: Convention Press, 1982.

Sisemore, John T. *Church Growth Through the Sunday School.* Nashville: Broadman Press, 1983.

Sisemore, John T. *How to Involve Unenrolled Church Members in Bible Study.* Nashville: Convention Press, 1988.

Smith, Sid. *Reaching the Black Community Through the Sunday School.* Nashville: Convention Press, 1984.

Spooner, Bernard M. and Harry M. Piland. *The People Challenge: Sunday School Outreach.* Nashville: Convention, 1985.

Sunday School Plan Book (annual). Nashville: Convention Press.

Vacation Bible School, Backyard Bible Club, and Mission Vacation Bible School materials can be ordered from Baptist Book Stores or by calling 1-800-458-BSSB.

CHAPTER 3

Discipleship: Supporting Personal Growth

Robert Holley

Robert Holley is director, Church Training Department, Arkansas Baptist State Convention, Little Rock, Arkansas.

Two pastors, Howard and Frank, were talking with each other at the Monday morning pastor's conference. Howard mentioned the large number of persons who had been saved in his church during the past six months. Frank asked how much attendance had increased at Howard's church. After all, with that many people being saved, surely attendance had skyrocketed. Howard hesitated to respond, but then admitted that attendance had grown very little. The reason was that his church was doing a poor job of discipling these many new converts. Most of them had attended church regularly for eight or ten weeks after becoming Christians. But then, their attendance became spasmodic.

What makes a single-staff church unique? I could give many answers to that question, but an important one is that the church will look to the pastor as the person who most can help them grow as Christians.

The pastor has numerous opportunities to help his church members grow in their faith: his weekly preaching, his Bible teaching, his example, his encouragement. However, the pastor of a single-staff church must ask himself this question: Does my vision for my church include a vision of my role as an equipper? One way for the pastor to accept his responsibility as an equipper is to give strong leadership for an effective Church Training program.

A church's training ministry takes its mandate from the Bible (Matt. 28:19-20; Eph. 4:11-16; Luke 14:27,33; John 8:31; Phil. 3:13-14). Each of us begins the Christian life as a babe in Christ. Our continued growth as a disciple is essential for our spiritual maturity. Church Training plays a major role in helping Christians move on toward spiritual maturity.

What Is the Work of Church Training?

To train disciples, Church Training seeks to carry out six tasks:

1. *Reach persons for discipleship training.*—Growth in discipleship is not optional for a Christian. Providing the kind of training that will help produce this spiritual growth is not optional for a church, either. We must aggressively seek to involve church members in discipleship training.

2. *Orient new church members for responsible church membership.*—When a person comes forward to join your church at the invitation time of the worship service, your responsibility to that person has only begun. We must help new members understand the meaning of conversion and church membership, nurture them in their Christian growth, help them understand basic doctrines of our faith, and introduce them to the life and work of the church they have joined.

3. *Equip church members for discipleship and personal ministry.*—Every church must lead its members to grow in their discipleship. This inner, personal growth is a life-long process for the Christian. In addition, believers must be equipped for ministry and shown how to use their God-given gifts to help build up the church.

4. *Teach Christian theology and Baptist doctrine, Christian ethics, Christian history, and church polity and organization.*—This is

the teaching task of Church Training and involves four important content areas. Simply stated, they have to do with what we believe, how we behave, who we are, and how we do our work. No Christian will grow in his or her discipleship without knowledge in these four areas.

5. *Train church leaders for ministry.*—Your church never will have enough leaders—persons who can provide leadership for your church's various programs and ministries. Church Training can help train these needed leaders.

6. *Interpret and undergird the work of the church and the denomination.*—The Church Training program, as well as all church programs, should give support to the entire church's ministry. Church Training should undergird the church's efforts in outreach, evangelism, stewardship, missions, worship, and ministry. It should keep members informed about the program of the church and the life and work of the denomination.

The approach you take in developing a Church Training program in your church will depend on several factors—size of your church, available resources, space, and availability of trained leaders. Your approach can range from an adult group, meeting periodically or continuously, led principally by the pastor, to a fully age-graded program offering continuing training opportunities weekly for all ages. Where possible, you will want to meet the needs of each age group. Training is most effective when others are enlisted and equipped to be the leaders and when it speaks to the needs and interests of each age group in the church.

What Is the Pastor's Role in Discipleship Training?
I suppose you can take two approaches to getting things done in a church—do it yourself or get someone else to do it. As a single-staff pastor, you will want to rely on both of these approaches. Let me explain.

Equip other people to be leaders of new member training, church member training, and leader training. And some of these training events you might need to lead yourself. Your personal involvement will allow you to fulfill your role as an equipper plus provide a model for the church family, so that in time, responsible volunteers will assume the tasks.

How can you, the pastor of a single-staff church, give leadership to a program of training?

1. *Help shape the church's training program.*—Lead the church to determine its training needs. Involve the whole church,

or at least the Church Council, in needs discovery.

After the church has determined training needs, it will need to decide on the organization. Some of your training will be special-needs training. Other training will be ongoing. You will also conduct some training on special occasions. These types of training all demand some kind of organizational structure.

2. *Lead your church to enlist and train leaders.*—The number and kinds of leaders you need will depend on the organizational structure the church has chosen. Work closely with your church's nominating committee to discover and enlist leaders who demonstrate commitment and potential. After leaders have been enlisted, provide training for them. Printed materials are available for these persons to read and study. You can have training workshops in your own church for these leaders. Your association will provide several training opportunities for them. Personnel from your state convention office would welcome the opportunity to help you train your church's leaders. The Baptist Sunday School Board provides excellent training at Ridgecrest and Glorieta Baptist Conference Centers.

3. *Guide in the selection of appropriate curriculum materials.*— Printed materials are a must for effective training. Our denomination provides basically two types of printed curriculum materials: dated study materials and undated study materials.

Dated materials include quarterlies for the various age groups who will be trained. Periodicals, member books, teacher books, and teaching helps are available. These dated materials are designed to be used on particular Sundays of the year.

Undated materials are published for use anytime there is a need or interest in the subject. These materials come primarily in three formats. *Equipping Center Modules* are available in six broad subject areas: evangelism and missions, Christian doctrine, family life, leadership, Christian growth, and church and community. These modules are designed primarily for adults and can be used in a variety of settings—short-term adult groups, week-night study, retreats, individual study, Wednesday night studies, and others.

The Church Study Course consists of hundreds of short-term studies of books in many different subject areas. These books can be used for individual study, group study, or as a supplement to dated materials.

LIFE (Lay Institute for Equipping) is a planned educational system that enables church members to grow at their own pace and to develop competencies in ministry according to their own goals and spiritual gifts. LIFE courses last approximately thirteen weeks and require participants to spend thirty minutes to an hour a day in preparation for weekly sessions. Two outstanding studies in this area are Parenting by Grace and Covenant Marriage.

The resource page at the end of this chapter provides instructions for ordering dated and undated materials.

Which Special Projects Can Help Train Your Members?

Your church's Church Training program hopefully will offer ongoing, weekly discipleship training opportunities for all age groups in your church. In addition, some special projects will provide you with discipleship training opportunities. Some of these special projects provide you, the pastor, with an opportunity for personal involvement.

1. *Dynamic Doctrines.*—This emphasis is a two-month doctrinal study offered for adults, youth, and children using the dated periodicals during October and November each year. These age groups will study the same doctrinal theme(s) for these two months, allowing you to have a churchwide emphasis on doctrine study for all family members. The doctrine study themes change each year.

2. *Missions emphases.*—The dated periodicals feature special missions studies for children, youth, and adults during the month of December each year. Also, each fifth Sunday study in the dated periodicals is a mission study. So, if your church uses the dated periodicals, all age groups in your church can receive training in missions education.

3. *Baptist Doctrine Study.*—Each year, our denomination sponsors an annual doctrine study. Member books and teaching materials are available for this emphasis. The suggested time for this doctrinal study is during Baptist Doctrine Study Week in April. But your church can schedule this emphasis at any time.

Some pastors choose to teach the doctrinal study book. Others enlist an outside teacher. Many pastors teach the book on Wednesday nights, while others preach series of sermons on the particular doctrine to be studied.

4. *Pastor's Seminar.*—In this approach, a pastor teaches one of the Equipping Center modules in an effort to enlist adults for discipleship training. The Pastor's Seminar can help reach adults who normally are not involved in Church Training.

5. *New Christian Encourager Plan.*—This approach to new

member training involves enlisting encouragers who work with new Christians in a one-to-one basis. Encouragers may also be trained to assist in decision counseling with those who make commitments at the invitation time during worship services.

6. *Potential leader training.*—Most single-staff churches experience great difficulty in locating enough trained leaders to staff the various church programs. Here is a plan that will help meet this need. Many church members feel inadequate, lacking the confidence to serve as leaders. The potential leader training course is designed for twenty-six weeks of study. The course covers a study of the biblical basis of leadership, an overview of the Bible, a study of Baptist doctrines, an overview of the total church program, and an introduction to leadership skills. The pastor can lead this course or enlist someone else to lead it.

7. *Reclaiming inactive members.*—I suppose at times, all churches have to give attention to this matter of reclaiming inactive church members. This task is not a study, but a project. Train persons in your church who will contact, visit, and encourage inactive members. For many single-staff churches, ministry with inactive members is an excellent deacon project.

8. *MasterLife discipleship training.*—MasterLife is a twenty-six week, in-depth discipleship training course for church members. The study is led by a qualified instructor. This lengthy study covers six essential Christian disciplines.

9. *DiscipleYouth.*—DiscipleYouth I and DiscipleYouth II are thirteen week studies for youth grades seven through twelve. The first course, DiscipleYouth I, involves thirteen weeks of study followed by thirteen weeks of witness training and visitation. DiscipleYouth II helps youth witness to and disciple other youth. These two studies will work in all sizes of churches.

No church will attempt to do all these emphases during any one year. However, you might find that some of these emphases really do address some needs in your church right now. Involve others in evaluating these approaches to training and discipleship.

The Church Training program should not be viewed as yet another demanding drain on the pastor's time and energy. The Church Training program can be a pastor's ally, the vehicle for expressing a large measure of his equipping ministry.

Resources

Buchanan, Edward A. *Developing Leadership Skills.* Nashville: Convention Press, 1971.

Church Training Magazine, Church Literature Dated Form.

Church Training Plan Book (annual). Nashville: Convention Press.

Edgemon, Roy and Arthur H. Criscoe. *A Biblical Model for Training Leaders.* Nashville: Convention Press, 1985.

Edgemon, Roy, compiler. *Discipleship Training: a Church Training Manual.* Nashville: Convention Press, 1986.

Edgemon, Roy. *Equipping Disciples Through Church Training.* Nashville: Convention Press, 1981.

Hobbs, Herschel H. *Baptist Faith and Message.* Nashville: Convention Press, 1971.

Order Dated Church Training periodicals, LIFE courses, and other Church Training resources by calling 1-800-458-BSSB.

CHAPTER 4

Missions: Moving Beyond Ourselves

Charles Farr

Charles Farr is associate pastor, Heritage Baptist Church, Colorado Springs, Colorado.

From its beginning days, our congregation wanted to be a Southern Baptist church. The church stated its objective—to embrace the values of Bible study, training, and mission action and ministry. The members of our church showed determination and they exhibited enthusiasm. Our resources, though, were meager.

The church met in a rented house for Bible study and worship. The nearby neighbors did not approve of our meeting in the house because our members' cars congested the already crowded street. But, our church grew, and we moved to a rented public school building.

Most of us pastors measure a church's effectiveness by the church's growth or lack of growth. When our church (a mission church in Colorado) was barely five years old, it was recognized as being among the top two percent of Southern Baptist churches with the most consistent numerical growth during the period 1975-79.

I want to organize the material in this chapter around our story. The story of our church is an example of how a single-staff church can do missions.

How does a mission church grow from thirty-eight members to more than one hundred members during its first year? I believe that question can be answered in two ways. First, our church emphasized basic programs. That's right! From its initial days, our church had age-graded Sunday School and Church Training programs. We provided classes for all ages. Yes, the numbers of people in our classes were few. But the organization was in place for outreach and for training our members and converts.

Both our Sunday morning and Sunday evening worship services featured music and preaching. In addition, we organized the Brotherhood and Woman's Missionary Union programs from our church's beginning days. Our people responded well to Brotherhood and WMU. These two organizations emphasized missions education with "hands on" mission action experiences. (I will describe some of these experiences later in this chapter.)

The second factor that contributed to our church's growth was the radiant spirit of our congregation. The pastor, deacons, teachers, and other leaders carried the love of Jesus into the homes of prospects, into work settings, and into the schools. Isn't ministry most effective when people offer it in the spirit of love and with a smiling face?

A Biblical Model

I believe Jesus gave us a model for missions and ministry when He stated these three commands: "Come unto me . . . learn of me . . . follow me" (Matt. 11:28,29; 4:19).

First, we "come" to Jesus in repentance, seeking forgiveness for our sin. This command by our Lord emphasizes the priority of evangelism.

Second, we "learn" from Jesus. This command emphasizes discipleship. The words *disciple* and *discipline* come from the same root word. The focus is on the pupil as well as on the subject being taught. When Jesus said, "Learn of me," He gave us a curriculum for life. Without discipleship training believers are left to wander.

Third, we "follow" Jesus. This command emphasizes a life-style of ministry. The emphasis here is on devotion to the things of God.

The missions task of a single-staff church must highlight each of these three concerns. Through missions, we evangelize the lost. We then educate our converts about the purpose and mission of the church. And we train these new Christians to minister to the needs of people. In short, the missions tasks of a church help us develop church members-ministers who live their Christian faith in the marketplace.

How Missions Helped Our Church

I am aware that many single-staff churches do not have large memberships. And many of these churches face real needs— they must finance church facilities, they need trained leaders, they must develop church programs, they have prospects to visit and members that need ministry. How can single-staff churches meet these challenges?

We discovered that the more our church did missions, the stronger we became in attendance, finances, ministry, and spirit. Before our church celebrated its first birthday, we had taught regular missions studies. These studies showed our people their need to be involved in missions. The result was that we sent several of our members on a mission tour in Haiti. Even though our church was receiving financial assistance from our association and state convention, we were sharing what we could by giving through the Cooperative Program and also by giving to a mission point in Haiti.

Our pastor's salary package was supplemented by money provided by our Home Mission Board. This assistance helped our church see firsthand the values of the Cooperative Program. By the end of our second year, however, we no longer needed pastoral aid monies. In fact, the total of our missions offerings during our church's third year of ministry, exceeded the total of all our receipts during our first year as a church. To me, that fact is evidence for the importance of a single-staff church emphasizing missions.

As our congregation grew from thirty-eight members to more than three hundred members in five years, the church had developed a simple program formula: Bible study, training, and missions education and mission action.

Missions in Our Biblical and Denominational Heritage

Missions originated in the heart of God. The human predicament was sin. Through the Redeemer, the Lord Jesus, God would save repentant sinners. God chose a people who were to be on mission for Him. Their mission was to spread God's Word and to be a blessing to other people. God's mandate was clear: disciple all nations, lead persons to become followers of Jesus Christ.

God's plan for worldwide missions is still being carried out today. The people in our churches need to know about modern-day missions work.

Southern Baptists always have been a people committed to missions. Our churches have been involved in missions to their respective communities and have cooperated with other Southern Baptist churches to minister to the needs of people around the world.

Our denomination's missions work is achieved through direct missions and through representative missions. *Direct missions* refers to the missions work done by a local church—proclaiming the gospel to the lost, ministering to persons in need, establishing new churches. *Representative missions* refers to the missions work done by churches through representative agents, namely missionaries. Southern Baptists have associational and state missionaries as well as missionaries appointed by our home and foreign mission boards. These career and short-term missionaries come from Southern Baptist churches and do the missions work that a single church could not do by itself.

Southern Baptist churches work together to do missions through the Cooperative Program, special missions offerings, and personal participation in missions. Hundreds of church members volunteer each year to work at home and abroad for short-term missions service. Other persons serve as missionaries for periods of one to two years.

Since career and volunteer missionaries represent our churches, our churches have the responsibility for supporting these individuals and their work.

Support for missions work involves three essentials: prayer support, personnel support, and financial support. We Southern Baptists cooperatively provide financial support for our world missions causes through our Cooperative Program giving. Additional financial support is provided by special missions offerings, such as the Lottie Moon Christmas Offering for Foreign Missions, the Annie Armstrong Easter Offering for Home Missions, and various state missions offerings.

Representative missionaries come from our churches. These persons have been nurtured spiritually in a Southern Baptist church. They learn missions concepts, Bible knowledge, and ministry skills through the training they receive at church.

A point of application comes from this fact. Reinforcement for missions is always needed. New missionaries will not be called from our churches unless each church provides an environment in which persons can hear and respond to God's call to missions. Therefore, missions education is a must. Our church members must know what Southern Baptists are doing in home and foreign missions work.

Church members' knowledge of missions must include biblical understandings about missions, the needs in the church's community, the needs in America and around the world, and what is happening today on various mission fields.

With this knowledge, and a Spirit-led desire to be obedient to Christ's Great Commission, church members can become involved in missions—locally through mission action projects and personal witnessing, and through volunteering for short-term home and foreign missions projects.

Missions Organizations for Our Churches

Do I have to remind you that the members of our churches won't promote or support missions causes automatically? Church members don't just become involved in missions in some sort of mystical way. What churches must do is organize themselves to provide programming that creates a climate for missions commitment. How can this be done?

Southern Baptists have two basic missions programs— Woman's Missionary Union (WMU) and Brotherhood. These two program organizations are flexible enough in their structure that even the smallest church can have a WMU and Brotherhood.

Church members who give leadership to the WMU and Brotherhood programs teach missions to fellow church members. Through this teaching, church members grow in their understanding of God's missionary purpose, with the result that many of these church members will become involved directly in mission projects and personal witnessing.

The curriculum for this missions education includes the missionary message of the Bible, the progress of Christian missions, and contemporary missions. A major emphasis is given on support of missions causes through the three channels of prayer, financial giving, and personal involvement.

Tithing is cited as the biblical way to support missions financially. The church's budget offerings, giving through the Cooperative Program, and special missions offerings are three channels for financial support of missions work.

The Brotherhood program provides missions education for men and boys. The WMU program provides missions education for women, girls, and preschool children. Both Brotherhood and WMU lead the church to accomplish its missions tasks. Common approaches by both organizations allow for joint work by the two organizations in such areas as churchwide missions projects. Mission action materials provide help for ministering to such groups as troubled families, alcoholics, drug abusers, military personnel, migrants, the aging, persons in institutions, and prisoners.

The work of WMU and Brotherhood is coordinated through the Church Council. The church-elected directors of WMU and Brotherhood serve as members of the Church Council.

Woman's Missionary Union

Woman's Missionary Union was founded in 1888. Throughout its history, some unchanging principles have helped focus the work of WMU. For instance, Alice Armstrong, sister of Annie Armstrong, once wrote: "Mission boards need money and women's (mission) organizations make money." WMU popularized tithing among Southern Baptists with massive tithing campaigns from 1920 to 1960. Early WMU leaders provided the nudge needed to guide our churches to include missions monies in their budgets.

At the time of her death, Annie Armstrong said: "After the study of God's Word comes the study of the fields." By 1906 the study of missions had become a primary promotional strategy of WMU. Today, the missions education provided through WMU is seen as an essential part of a church's curriculum.

Early pioneers in WMU often referred to our career missionaries as "our substitutes." This warm feeling between the sender and the ones sent have made WMU an electrifying force for the financial support of "our substitutes."

WMU leaders know financial support alone is not enough.

Prayer provides the spiritual lifeline for reaching the world for Christ.

The Woman's Missionary Union in a church has these tasks:
- Teach missions.
- Engage in mission action and personal witnessing.
- Support missions.
- Interpret and undergird the work of the church and the denomination.

How can a smaller membership church begin a WMU? At least two options are possible. The first would be a one-woman WMU. In this approach, a woman in the church would assume the role of WMU director. She would learn about missions herself and then help involve the church in missions. A second approach would be for the church to begin several age-level WMU groups for women, girls, and preschool children. The number of age-level groups would depend on the church's size.

Here are the possible age-level groups:
- Mission Friends for preschool boys and girls;
- Girls in Action for girls in grades one through six;
- Acteens for girls in grades seven through twelve;
- Baptist Young Women for women ages eighteen through twenty-nine; and
- Baptist Women for women ages thirty and up.

WMU provides printed materials in the form of missions magazines for each of these age-level groups. Training manuals and other leadership materials are available. These resources can be ordered from Woman's Missionary Union offices in Birmingham, Alabama.

A single-staff church can combine or adapt any of the WMU age-level groups as needed. For example, all women in the church could be in a Baptist Women's group.

Workers in the church's WMU should be elected by the church. Working with the pastor and the Church Council, if there is one, these workers might consider two primary projects during their first year of work: (1) observing the Weeks of Prayer for Home and Foreign Missions, and encouraging financial giving to the related missions offerings; and (2) conducting annual missions studies of the foreign missions and home missions study books for the year. Resources are available to help a church with these two projects.

When the church's WMU organization has grown some, quarterly missions studies or missions projects could be held. From this quarterly emphasis could come the development of various age-level groups and a broader program of missions education and missions involvement. And, sometimes, one or two age-level groups can be organized even if the church has no WMU director.

Brotherhood
Involving men and boys in missions is a must for every church. As with WMU, this involvement could begin with only two or three boys or men or with a fully age-graded program.

Here are the tasks of the Brotherhood organization:
• Engage in mission activities.
• Teach missions.
• Pray for and give to missions.
• Develop personal ministry.
• Interpret and undergird the work of the church and the de-nomination.

When involving men and boys in missions keep these truths in mind:
• The needs of boys and men are a primary consideration, though some kind of formal organization might develop later.
• Large numbers of men and boys are not needed to begin a Brotherhood.
• Effectiveness isn't measured only by the number of meetings held.
• Meetings are not the end; they are only a means to the end.
• What is best for one church might not be best for your church.
• Although you might start with only a few boys or men, your goals should be to lead all men and boys in your church to be involved in missions.

One meaningful thing a Brotherhood organization will do for your church is to lift high the biblical teachings regarding the "people of God." The Bible makes no distinctions between clergy and laity. All Christians are ministers. Brotherhood will reinforce this Bible teaching.

From its beginning, Brotherhood has been a missions educa-tion organization that encourages men and boys to be God's Kingdom citizens. This encouragement is given through printed Brotherhood materials. The ultimate goal sought is not just infor-mation about missions, but involvement in missions.

By definition, missions education is what Brotherhood does to qualify men and boys for missions involvement. Typical Brotherhood mission activities include mission action projects, personal evangelism, mass evangelism, and special mission projects. Through these kinds of events, the Brotherhood organization leads men and boys to minister and witness to people.

Your church could begin a Brotherhood by using a one-man Brotherhood approach. Then, as the other possibilities develop, leaders can be enlisted for Baptist Men, Baptist Young Men, High School Baptist Young Men, and Royal Ambassadors.

Curriculum materials for all these groups is provided through the Brotherhood Commission in Memphis, Tennessee. The Commission will provide your church with a Brotherhood starter kit and basic materials at a reduced price. Free materials to help the men and boys in your church to understand what the Brotherhood organization is are available on request from the Brotherhood Commission.

Your Church and the Cooperative Program

Southern Baptist churches experience spiritual blessings as they decide to give certain percentages of their financial receipts through the Cooperative Program. How does such an approach work?

A church begins by providing information to members about the Cooperative Program. Printed materials can be ordered free of charge from any state convention stewardship office.

A church votes to give a certain portion of its receipts through the Cooperative Program. The percentage amount can be whatever the church chooses.

The church's percentage amount is sent each month to the state convention's offices. A portion of this amount will be retained by the state for missions ministries in the state. The remainder of the money is then sent to the Southern Baptist Executive Committee for world missions causes and for the support of many denominational boards and agencies (the Sunday School Board and Woman's Missionary Union do not receive Cooperative Program support).

How is this money used to support world missions? At the annual Southern Baptist Convention meeting, the messengers approve an annual Cooperative Program budget. The Foreign and Home Mission Boards receive about half of their budgets from Cooperative Program monies given by the churches. Our six Southern Baptist seminaries receive funding from the Cooperative Program. The work of denominational agencies such as the

Historical Commission, the Education Commission, and the Christian Life Commission are supported through Cooperative Program funds. In all, some twenty denominational boards and agencies receive SBC Cooperative Program funds.

What is the value of Cooperative Program giving to the local church? One, the church is blessed by its participation in financial giving to worldwide missions causes. Two, by cooperating with other churches, the church is able to do much more for missions than it could by itself. Three, members have the joy of knowing their tithes and offerings are being put to work in Kingdom causes. Four, the ministries of thousands of Southern Baptist missionaries are supported.

State and National Missions Offerings

Your state convention probably sponsors an annual state missions offering. In addition, your church is encouraged each year to give to the two national missions offerings: the Lottie Moon Christmas Offering for Foreign Missions and the Annie Armstrong Easter Offering for Home Missions.

These annual offerings give your church an opportunity to extend itself in missions involvement at home and abroad. Most churches find that the congregation's enthusiasm for the two national offerings is elevated when mission studies are taught prior to the offering emphases. Each year, books are designated as the study books for these two offering emphases.

Your church could sponsor a missions banquet prior to these offering weeks. Enlist a speaker who will motivate your people to give generously. The WMU and Brotherhood programs take the lead in promoting congregational support of the state and national missions offerings.

New Missions

Who starts new churches? Some people would answer that questions by saying only established or big churches can start new churches. Others would say that only debt-free churches should start a new church. Both responses are incorrect.

While our church was still the "new kid on the block," we were challenged to sponsor a mission. Another denomination owned a desirable tract of land in a growing subdivision. The denomination had no plans for this land. With financial assistance from the Home Mission Board, we acquired the land and began a new church. Your church can experience the blessing of mothering a new church or mission.

Missions Projects

During a World Missions Conference in our church, we heard a Southern Baptist missionary to Tanzania tell about the needs of pastors and churches in that country. Among the many needs were metal roofs to replace the grass roofs on Tanzanian Baptist church buildings. Our people got excited about the idea of adopting one of those churches for a reroofing project. As a matter of fact, our church ended up providing metal roofs for seven churches.

As I shared earlier, our church was involved in a mission trip to Haiti. We ministered among the rural and mountain people there. We provided technical assistance with food production, several village preaching points, and some environmental restoration. In addition, we provided medical supplies for a nurse's station situated among thirty thousand people. During a four-year period, our church's members went to Haiti to serve in various ministry roles, including a series of revival meetings in the local churches.

Our church was blessed beyond measure by such an experience. If your church would benefit from such hands-on mission work, contact our Home and Foreign Mission Boards for information. Again, WMU and Brotherhood are the major vehicles for this kind of ministry.

Your Church's Mission Strategy

Give priority to these areas:

1. Enlist and train leaders for WMU and Brotherhood, even if you only work with two or three persons in the beginning.

2. Develop a churchwide plan for missions education and mission action.

3. Enlarge and staff your WMU and Brotherhood organizations as growth possibilities increase.

4. Lead your people to cooperate with other Baptist churches in addressing missions concerns. A primary way for doing this is by giving through the Cooperative Program. Through such giving, your church will develop a world view.

Resources

Brock, Charles. *The Principles and Practice of Indigenous Church Planting.* Nashville: Broadman Press, 1981.

The Church Missions Committee, Undated Materials Order Form.

Miles, Delos. *Evangelism and Social Involvement.* Nashville: Broadman Press, 1986.

Padilla, Concepcion. *The Challenge of Reaching Language Persons for Bible Study.* Nashville: Convention Press, 1986.

Redford, F. J. *Planting New Churches.* Nashville: Broadman Press, 1979.

The Commission, Foreign Mission Board of the Southern Baptist Convention.

Missions USA, Home Mission Board of the Southern Baptist Convention.

Willis, Avery. *Biblical Basis of Missions.* Nashville: Convention Press, 1979.

Baptist Brotherhood, Brotherhood Commission of the Southern Baptist Convention.

Brotherhood Notebook, Brotherhood Commission of the Southern Baptist Convention.

Church Brotherhood Planbook, Brotherhood Commission of the Southern Baptist Convention.

Mission Activities for Men and Boys, Brotherhood Commission of the Southern Baptist Convention.

Training Brotherhood Leaders, Brotherhood Commission of the Southern Baptist Convention.

Allen, Catherine. *A Century to Celebrate: History of WMU.* Birmingham, AL: Woman's Missionary Union, 1987.

Baptist Women Manual, Birmingham, AL: Woman's Missionary Union, 1987.

Edwards, Judith L. *How to Pray for Missions,* Birmingham, AL: Woman's Missionary Union, 1987.

Sorrill, Bobbie. *WMU—a Church Missions Organization.* Birmingham, AL: Woman's Missionary Union, 1981.

◆ **CHAPTER 5** ◆

Administration: Protecting the Fellowship

D. G. McCoury

D. G. McCoury is consultant for pastoral ministries, single-staff church, and the associational program of Pastoral Ministries, Church Administration Department, Baptist Sunday School Board.

I remember well a single-staff church in a state convention I served. Regularly, that church was recognized at the annual state evangelism conference. This church consistently led our state convention in baptisms. I noticed an interesting fact about the church. While it led the state convention in baptisms, its yearly average Sunday School attendance never increased. The pastor of this church certainly had compassion for the lost. He modeled personal witnessing and led his church to do effective outreach and evangelism. Yet, the church failed to keep its many converts.

Another church I recall majored on training and disci-

pleship. The pastor attended numerous seminars to improve his skills in church member training. The church's program was slanted heavily toward discipleship training. But this church had so turned inward that it did a poor job of outreach and evangelism.

Sometimes, situations like these two exist in a church simply because the church is concentrating so heavily in one area of biblical growth that the church neglects the other areas of growth. Why is this so?

Many churches do not see church growth in all four areas (evangelistic, discipleship, missions, and administrative growth). These two churches had not done an adequate job with their administration issue.

I often hear pastors say, "God did not call me to be an administrator." Yet the Bible says: "If God has given you . . . administrative ability, take the responsibility seriously" (Rom. 12:8, TLB). Did you ever consider that good administration is just another way to minister effectively?

Church growth calls for the practice of good administration. For example, if the church is growing numerically, certain administrative actions are a must.

• New church member orientation should be provided.
• Discipleship training is needed by the new converts.
• Many new members must become involved in various places of service. This means some of these people will need training for the areas of service for which they volunteer.
• The church's organization will need to be enlarged to accommodate the growth.
• Additional meeting space may need to be provided.

An Organized Organism

Ministry is effective only when the work of various organizations and programs is coordinated well. Church programs are interdependent and interrelated; they constantly interact with one another. Every church, regardless of its size, has Divine work to do. Organization is needed to do this work effectively. How much organization is needed depends on the church's resources and needs. Even smaller membership churches should organize for effectiveness.

Structures must be provided for each church program. Those programs all need trained leaders. All churches need a clear understanding of their mission. They need to be led to set ministry goals. They must plan, organize, and evaluate their work. Quality communication is a must. Good administration helps churches accomplish these kinds of tasks.

The number of programs in your church will vary according to your church's size, needs, and available resources. In Southern Baptist life, six basic programs and numerous service and emphasis programs are available for churches to use (see page 26).

The kind of organization and number of programs your church has depends also on your church's interpretation of its nature and mission. The church's Divine commission (Matthew 28:19-20) is unchanging. While a church does have freedom to organize its work around its mission, a church does not have the freedom to organize its work apart from its mission.

Again, my point is that your church may choose to organize itself in whatever way your congregation sees best. The number of programs your church has will be decided by the size of your congregation and available resources. Smaller membership churches need not try to copy the organization and program choices of larger, multiple-staff churches.

Administration Is Ministry

The mission of your church is accomplished by your members, and not by programs. Programs are tools. The work of your church must be both inward (to itself) and outward (to others). Christ established the church, but human beings create and operate its institutional forms. Your church's organization and/or structure can enhance your church's work or hinder your church's work. Your church should provide enough organization and programming that all the members can find places to use their gifts in the work of the church.

As I talk about administration, I want you to realize I am speaking foremost about ministry, not just methods or organizations or policies. We must administrate, not manipulate, the church's "people process" and help the church use its resources well. A healthy church, organized and functioning, recognizes the purpose of its programs is to grow people.

Church administration involves procedures and techniques that can be learned by study and practice. *As an art,* church administration calls for sensitivity to people, intuitive judgement, and good timing. *As a science,* church administration involves principles of leadership and management. The art and science of church administration can be learned. Available to pastoral ministers are numerous conferences and seminars to help them improve or learn administrative skills.

Administrative Services

Administrative services assist the church to plan its program, manage its resources, and govern its life and work. To *plan* means to determine a mode of operation and a course of action. To *manage* means to administer or carry on the business affairs of the church as requested or assigned. To *govern* means to guide and/or direct and refers to those means by which a church regulates or rules its affairs.

In Southern Baptist life, a common practice is to assign responsibilities for administrative work to the pastor, general church officers, church committees, and the Church Council. Each church decides which officers, committees, and councils it needs. Typically, churches call a pastor, select deacons, and elect volunteer leaders to enable the church to do its work effectively.

A Biblical Example of Church Administration

When we read Acts 6 we are made aware that, as the early church grew numerically, some functional tasks were not being taken care of well (some widowed persons were being neglected in the daily administration of food). At this point in time, the early church had limited organizational structure, if any at all.

Because this problem (the neglect of some widowed persons) threatened the church's fellowship, the apostles assembled the church body to discuss options. The church decided to select seven persons to handle the matter.

Here is a good example of church administration. A need arose (widowed persons needed food). An organizational method was chosen (seven men were selected to handle this ministry need).

Administrative Actions

Every church must deal with several administrative responsibilities:

• The church must govern its life and work under the lordship of Christ.

• The church must determine which programs it will have.

• The church must establish some kind of organizational form to conduct and/or coordinate its various programs and services.

• The church must decide how it will cooperate with other churches.

• The church must establish and maintain certain external relationships with its community.

• The church will need to call a pastor and elect volunteer leaders and then assign responsibilities to these individuals.

• The church must provide and allocate resources for its work.

These actions represent work that must be performed regularly by the church family if the church is to move forward. These responsibilities are administrative in nature; that is, they have to do with the overall guidance of the church's life. These various administrative responsibilities are often delegated by the church to the pastor, the deacons, committees, church officers, or councils. These persons or groups do not usurp the authority of the church, but aid its life and work (nor should any of these persons or groups usurp the work of other persons or groups).

The Pastor's Role

The pastor of a single-staff church often is assigned the responsibility for certain administrative actions. The pastor provides "process" leadership that guides the church in the right direction. One way he does this is by promoting the personal growth and development of deacons and church program leaders and by sharing in their efforts to improve the church's program, its outreach, its ministry of care, and its missions ministry. The word *leadership* often has been defined as the process of influencing the activities of an individual or group toward the accomplishment of a goal in a given situation. This definition contains three important words:

Influencing.—This is a good word for pastoral leadership. The pastor contributes to the discussions of church leaders, the Church Council, program councils, and church committees as they plan recommendations to the church. Through his preaching, the pastor is a persuader or influencer of people's thinking and behavior.

Accomplishment.—Churches hope to achieve something. Such churches are founded on common vision and shared goals. They have a strategy for reaching their goals.

Situation.—Situations are the conditions, circumstances, surroundings, and resources of that church. Churches find themselves in real situations. They must govern their work according to biblical truth, doctrinal distinctives, historical positions, and congregational identity.

Thus, the single-staff church pastor is a leader of leaders who share equipping responsibilities with him. Because the church has called him as pastor, selected its deacons, and elected volunteer leaders, the congregation has declared: We want the type of leaders who will help us be the church Christ intended us to be.

The pastor must be aware of theological guidelines for his work, must practice leadership principles, and accept responsibility for equipping church members. He must build a team of church members-ministers. That is among the most basic of his administrative responsibilities.

A wise pastor will multiply his ministry by equipping the church's leaders, who in turn, equip other church members. An example would be a pastor who, when he has equipped the Sunday School director, has set free that person to direct the church's Bible teaching team (all Sunday School workers). That team then provides outreach, Bible study, and ministry for the entire Sunday School roll. The pastor never could do this much by himself.

Leadership Skills

Because the pastor is such an influential person in the congregation, his leadership skills must show improvement in at least three skills areas:

People skills.—Strong human-relations skills are needed by all pastoral ministers. The ability to get along with people in the church is crucial. The inability to practice common courtesy, get along with people in the church, and become a team member can become the downfall of a pastor's ministry. Good people skills also become the basis for learning skills in delegation, conflict management, communication, motivation, and group dynamics.

Technical skills.—This leadership skill area involves the practice of ministry. Included in the practice of ministry are preaching, counseling, visitation, witnessing, teaching, and planning. All pastors can learn new skills in these areas, as well as improve present levels of skills in these areas.

Conceptual skills.—What is meant by "conceptual skills" is an understanding of various church programs and how each program can help the church fulfill its ministry. Without these conceptual skills, a pastor will be limited in his ability to help the church establish ministry goals and objectives.

A pastor will want to improve his understanding of the *basic* church programs. These programs are not separate identities in themselves. For example, Sunday School is the church reaching people for Bible study. Church Training is the church discipling its members. WMU and Brotherhood are the church teaching and practicing missions. The Music Ministry is the church at worship. Pastoral Ministries is the church proclaiming the gospel, caring for persons, and being led to accomplish its (the church's) mission. The single-staff pastor must develop conceptual abilities to see how these six basic church programs can help his church.

Many smaller membership churches will not have all six of these basic programs. Yet, even if one or more of these basic programs is not in a church, the tasks of that program are still "handles" for accomplishing that church's mission. Even if a church does not have a particular program, the church must find ways to carry out the tasks of that program. Let me give you an example.

A new church was begun in a western state. This church's average Sunday morning attendance was about forty persons. The church's limited meeting facilities only allowed for Sunday morning services. This congregation recognized the importance of reaching people and teaching them the Bible. So, this church had Sunday School and a morning worship service each Sunday.

This new church had no Church Training program, nor did they have a WMU or Brotherhood. Yet, the members of the church believed Baptist doctrine, as well as missions, needed to be taught to the members. Here is what this church did.

They ordered the October-November-December Church Training quarterlies because this quarter's material always contains doctrinal studies and missions studies. They planned a time for studying these periodicals. Thus, this church was able to supplement its Sunday School's Bible study task with doctrinal and missions studies.

This example is only one of how a church can do creative planning to discover ways to get at its mission. You don't always have to have several well-staffed, finely-tuned organizations and a certain "hour" to meet in order to accomplish the various tasks of the church.

One danger the single-staff pastor faces is that of becoming too much of a specialist. That is, he becomes competent in only one or two areas, say preaching and counseling. Other leadership roles such as delegation, planning, administration, visitation, or worship leadership are neglected. But the ability to "conceptualize" the total mission of the church is necessary for the pastor to see that all functions of the church are being carried out.

The Pastor as Leader of Leaders

Your vision for the church must include a vision for equipping your church's leaders. With this vision in mind, you truly can become the leader of leaders. In addition, you multiply your ministry effectiveness. A team of leaders can accomplish more than just the pastor himself can accomplish.

This team of leaders commonly is called the Church Council. It is made up of the chairperson of the deacons, Sunday School director, Church Training director, WMU director, music director, Brotherhood director, along with chairpersons from key committees. (Some churches also include several "at-large" members.) I know what some of you are thinking. You are saying to yourself: *Our church only has a deacon chairperson, Sunday School director and WMU director. So, we can't have a Church Council!*

Wait! Remember that earlier I talked about the need to develop those conceptual skills? Here is an example of how that skill is needed. You don't have to have every program leader previously mentioned to have a working Church Council. Start with what you have. I have worked with Church Councils that included only the deacon chairperson and the Sunday School director. And, I have had an active Church Council in a church that averaged less than fifty in weekly Sunday School attendance.

An Administrative Team

Your church needs a Church Council because this group of leaders can guide your church toward spiritual directions. This pathway will help your people develop the view that they truly are the people of God.

If you will spend a couple of hours each month with the Church Council, this administrative team will save you hours of work. Through the work of this team of church leaders, your church will be led to accomplish more of its mission. Resources for developing and working with a Church Council are listed at the end of this chapter.

The pastor's ability to work with a Church Council can be the difference between a growing church and one whose growth is at a standstill. By working with the members of the Church Council, you help strengthen the church programs each member represents. Stronger church programs mean a more spiritual ministry for your church. After all, spiritual ministries are achieved through effective church programs.

A strong pulpit ministry is needed. But think how much more

effective your pulpit ministry can be when backing it up are effective, volunteer-led programs that help the church grow in the areas of evangelism, discipleship, missions, and administration.

Multiplying Leaders
Working with the Church Council will multiply the single-staff church pastor's leadership effectiveness by:
• saving you time and keeping you in touch with church programs,
• maintaining an excellent system for congregational feedback,
• providing support among lay leaders, and
• providing a group of leaders who can help equip church members for ministry.

You say, "I'm convinced of the need for a Church Council. But what exactly does a Church Council do?"

First, the Church Council leads the church to define its mission. Every church needs a written statement of its mission or objectives for ministry. The Church Council can lead the church to develop such a written statement.

Second, the Church Council studies church and community needs and evaluates the congregation's response to those needs. Then, the Church Council recommends goals to meet priority needs. Plans are developed to meet goals. These plans then are calendered and submitted to the church for adoption.

Third, the Church Council meets regularly to coordinate and calendar church schedules and activities. At their regular meeting, Church Council members will evaluate the activities that occurred during the previous month. They will make sure plans are finalized for activities for the next month. Questions such as these will be asked: Are we ready for each event on next month's calendar? Do we have the resources in hand? Have needed persons been enlisted? Does everybody know what they are supposed to do? Is there something that hasn't been done?

At this same meeting, Church Council members will look toward the second and third coming months to make final plans for calendared activities. Many churches find helpful having a Church Council retreat or weekend planning meeting when the calendar of activities for the entire year is developed for recommendation to the church.

Setting the Course
With any church, planning is essential. The church's ministry plan

is the map which shows the church the direction it should go. A planned ministry allows the church to use the various gifts and talents of church members. The Church Council is the ideal group to help a church do its planning. The Church Council could consider using the Spiritual Directions Emphasis as a beginning point for planning (see resource page at end of this chapter).

Having every member of the church conduct studies, evaluate options, prepare plans, order resources, and manage those resources would not be practical in terms of time and work. So, a church elects program leaders, church officers, and church committee members to be its planning-coordinating-evaluating group.

The Church Council becomes the central link between calendared activities, church programs, workers in the various programs, church committees, and church officers.

The recommendations from the Church Council always are brought to the church for approval. That is essential for doing things the Baptist way, self-governing. The Church Council exists to serve the church.

How well are the program leaders, committee members, church officers, members of your church working together? Having an active, trained Church Council will enable your church's members to work together as they do the work of the church. This is why administration helps protect the fellowship of the church.

Church Constitution and By-Laws

Your church needs a document that spells out, in an orderly way, the procedure your church will take for certain key actions. Examples of these actions would be how members join your church, how deacons are selected, which programs your church will have and the functions of each, how many committees your church will have and the duties of each, and how congregational decision-making will occur.

A written constitution and by-laws is such a document. The *constitution* sets forth guiding doctrinal and biblical principles that govern your church. The *by-laws* portion gets down to the specifics of your church's polity: election procedures, church policies, church business, and so forth.

Two approaches can be taken when writing a constitution and by-laws. One approach is a "strict" approach. Every possible situation, action, or need is thought of and included in the document.

Very detailed instructions are given. The other approach is the "broad" approach. Here, general statements are made and broad instructions are given for each concern in the by-laws. Helps for writing a church constitution and by-laws can be received from the Church Administration Department of the Baptist Sunday School Board.

A pastor's ability to spend quality time with small groups of leaders is essential for his effectiveness. One way to do this is by using a Church Council to help see that essential administrative actions are handled and the church's fellowship protected.

In this chapter, I have been talking about administration. I hope you now have realized that what I really have been talking about is being the leader of a leadership team. Some pastors shriek when they hear the word *administration*. In the New Testament, the Greek word *kuberneseis* is translated "administration" (1 Cor. 12:28). The word describes the helmsman of a ship whose job it was to steer the ship safely toward the harbor.

Pastor, by doing a good job with church administration, you will guide well that ship called the church. Administrative work in the church is spiritual work, too. Effective administrative work protects the fellowship of the church.

Resources

Brown, Truman, Jr. *Church Council Handbook.* Nashville: Convention Press, 1981.

Brown, Truman, Jr. *Church Planning a Year at a Time.* Nashville: Convention Press, 1984.

Brown, Truman, Jr. *Minister's Personal Management Manual.* Nashville: Convention Press, 1988.

Brown, Truman, Jr. *How to Conduct a Spiritual Directions Emphasis: Retreat and Annual Planning Guide.* Nashville: Convention Press, 1986.

Church Administration, Church Literature Dated Form.

Church Officer and Committee Series Packet, Undated Materials Order Form.

Powers, Bruce P., editor. *Church Administration Handbook.* Nashville: Broadman Press, 1985.

Sheffield, James. *Church Officer and Committee Guidebook.* Nashville: Convention Press, 1976.

Tidwell, Charles A. *Church Administration-Effective Leadership for Ministry.* Nashville: Broadman Press, 1985.

Treadwell, William C. and Larry L. McSwain. *Church Organization Alive.* Nashville: Broadman Press, 1987.

◆ **CHAPTER 6** ◆

Worship: Encountering God

Bob Norman

Bob Norman is pastor, Clearview Baptist Church, Franklin, Tennessee.

Do you agree with this statement? "The first business of a church is not evangelism, nor missions, nor benevolence; it is worship. The worship of God and Christ should be at the center of all else that the church does."[1]

This statement from an outstanding Baptist churchman might lead us to believe that the main function of a church is to worship. But I believe the intent of the statement is that only Christians who have experienced the true spirit of Christ in worship are equipped to evangelize.

In other words, the emphasis can't be only on evan-

gelism, nor can the emphasis be only on worship. Both emphases are needed in a church. True worship is not just withdrawing from the world to be with God. True worship leads us to an encounter with Christ that prepares us to witness to the world.

In single-staff churches, worship is an important matter. Gary Farley has written: "Many small churches, if not most, see their primary function as worship. They come together for proclamation, prayer, and praise. Other activities may be seen as extraneous."[2]

Values of Worship
Worship is essential to the growth of a church. The church can't get along without effective, well-planned worship services. Some of the experiences that occur during worship services are vital to the life of a church. Among the values of congregational worship are the following:

• Worship brings us into the presence of God and gives us a sense of oneness with Him.

• Worship affords an opportunity for celebrating the joys and victories of Christian living.

• Worship helps fulfill the need for fellowship with other Christians.

• Worship helps us see our need for confession of sin and forgiveness.

• Worship provides comfort for the troubled heart.

• Worship deepens our understanding of the mysteries of our Christian faith.

• Worship invites commitment to Christian service and suggests channels for serving the Lord.

• Worship enables us to have a broader perspective of God's kingdom.

• Worship provides an opportunity for calling the lost to Christ.

In true worship, we experience the resurrected Christ amid the gathered church. Jesus said: "The true worshippers shall worship the Father in spirit and in truth: for the Father seeketh such to worship him" (John 4:23). God is seeking worshipers! Worship provides a means for human response to Divine initiative.

Reality in worship is found "in spirit and in truth." The Holy Spirit must touch the human spirit before true worship occurs. Singing, preaching, praying can lead us to worship, but true worship is more than any of these.

Worship enables us to praise God for who He is and to thank

Him for what He has done. The thanksgiving and praise we give to God in worship prepare us to serve Him in daily life.

Effective worship meets the needs of the congregation. In worship, the congregation senses God's presence and then responds to that presence in meaningful ways. Worship can take many different forms, but whatever the form, the worship of God is necessary.

Baptists and Worship

Historically, in Southern Baptist life, the Sunday morning worship service has served the church not only for worship, but also as a source of religious education. Let me explain. In worship, we sing doctrinal songs, we hear the Scriptures read, we listen as the Bible is interpreted with authority and pastoral sensitivity. In many single-staff churches, the pastor functions as the resident Christian educator.

The people in the pews need spiritual nourishment. Many of them only attend worship. They do not receive the benefits of the church's teaching and training programs. So the need today is for single-staff church pastors to give solid biblical content to their sermons. The preacher must not be caught up in entertaining the folks who have come to church, nor be graded on his communication skills, nor be seen as one who must produce for the spectators. Rather, with pastoral care, the preacher must open God's Word and apply it to the church family he lives with each day.

Many of our single-staff churches resist changes in the order of worship. I remember when I used to think the only way worship could begin was by the congregation standing and singing the Doxology.

Some single-staff churches will not have such worship props as choir robes, printed bulletins, public address systems, ornate pulpit furniture, or an organ. But the church doesn't need these props to be God's people on mission for Him.

A Personal Word

The church I pastor meets in a high school cafeteria with noon lunch menus in open view. Along the cafeteria walls are banners whose words cheer the school's athletic teams. Each week this sight helps me see people in a meaningful way. Think of the contrast between what Jesus saw and what His disciples saw. They cried, "Look, what wonderful stones. What wonderful buildings!" Jesus also said, "Look!" But when He said, "look" He was referring to people with needs. (See Mark 13:1 and Matthew 9:36-38.)

Our church began with a handful of people who met in the dining room of a house built in 1875. Our early discussions centered on the fear that we would "grow too much" and lose our spirit of openness and friendliness. But today the hallmark of our congregation might be called "informality with dignity."

Visitors to our services tell me our congregation reflects spiritual enthusiasm. A bivocational minister of music serves our church well. Through his leadership in worship, we experience God's presence each week.

Preaching in Worship

I have come to a time in my ministry when I want to.avoid what has been called "rocking horse preaching." This is the kind of preaching that constantly moves, but doesn't go anywhere; it charges, but never advances. In this type of preaching, the preacher's words sting, bite, and kick.

I believe preaching must, by the Holy Spirit's working, influence people to do something. The Bible proclaimed is what we need.

Most congregations would rate preaching at the top of a list of the pastor's various duties. The people know the importance of the pastor setting aside time for reading, reflection, prayer, study, and solid sermon preparation. The pastor occupies that unique role of one who stands before the people to proclaim "a message from the Lord." Regardless of the size of membership, all churches deserve well-prepared sermons.

Preaching is a major part of worship, but not the only part. Yet preaching must be effective. Some questions to help you evaluate the effectiveness of your preaching are:
- Is your preaching strongly biblical?
- Do your sermons speak directly to the needs of people?
- Do you use a planned program of preaching?
- Do you preach the great themes of the Christian faith?
- Is your sermon preparation bathed in prayer?
- When you preach, do you seek to be empowered by the Holy Spirit?

Music in Worship

Christianity is a singing religion! People love music, especially their own. The vitality of the church often is reflected in its singing. In the early days of the church, "singing and making melody in the heart to the Lord" seemed to have been characterized by spontaneity, simplicity, and sincerity.

In our church, our evening service on the second Sunday night of the month is called "Mostly Music." Our attendance on this night is double our normal Sunday evening attendance figures. Our own church members sing and play musical instruments. Sometimes, a guest musician is invited to share musically in this service.

Your church's Music Ministry allows many church members to use their talents to enhance worship services. These members' involvement in a ministry of music also helps them grow in their discipleship. Through musical experiences, some persons are led to life-long commitment to Jesus Christ and to responsible church membership.

Your church's Music Ministry makes a positive contribution to your church's life by: (1) helping church members discover and develop their musical talents, (2) using the ministry of music to inspire people to a closer walk with God, and (3) enhancing the quality of congregational worship.

A church can look to its Music Ministry to accomplish at least these five tasks:

• Provide musical experiences in congregational services.
• Provide church music education.
• Lead the church to witness and minister through music.
• Assist the church programs in providing training in musical skills and in consultation about musical equipment.
• Interpret and undergird the work of the church and the denomination.

Musical praise enhances our worship of God. Through music our emotions are brought into the act of worship. Emotions are a valid part of our worship. Paul counseled us to pray with the spirit and pray with the mind, sing with the spirit and sing with the mind (1 Cor. 14:15).

Through music we express our joy, our thanksgiving to God. More than forty recorded psalms command us to "sing unto the Lord." God calls for worship that involves our whole being. The body, mind, spirit, and emotions all should be laid on the altar of worship. Music is the dominant way we praise God in worship.

Worship and Your Church's Program of Pastoral Ministries
One task of the Pastoral Ministries program of your church is to proclaim the gospel to believers and unbelievers (see task statements on page 26). All Christians share the duty and privilege of

proclaiming the gospel. Really, all church programs should proclaim the gospel.

In two primary ways, the pastor of a single-staff church fulfills the "proclaiming" task of the Pastoral Ministries program: (1) lead and equip the church to witness and (2) plan and lead worship services in which the gospel is proclaimed.

The gospel can be proclaimed through public presentations, private conversations, and written communications. Preaching a sermon, observing the Lord's Supper and baptism, presenting the gospel in music, sharing personal testimonies, reading the Scriptures, presenting religious drama, and showing evangelistic films are just a few of the ways to proclaim the gospel to groups of persons.

The Pastoral Ministries task of proclaiming the gospel involves much more than just preaching sermons. Leading worship, witnessing personally, teaching God's Word, training persons in Bible skills are additional ways proclamation is done.

Worship experiences during Vacation Bible School, retreats, and camps are events which can help children and youth learn the importance of proclaiming the gospel.

A shopping center wall could serve as a screen for showing appropriate films for family members who wait. Parks, backyards, camping areas, and recreation centers provide additional places for sharing the gospel. The Church Recreation Department of the Baptist Sunday School Board provides services and printed materials to assist churches to proclaim the gospel in creative ways.

And, don't overlook deacons. Faithful, committed deacons work with the pastor in proclaiming the gospel. If you will train your church's deacons to proclaim the gospel, you will multiply the effectiveness of your church's evangelistic outreach.

The Single-Staff Pastor as Worship Leader
Too often, pastors emphasize their role as "preacher" but overlook their role as worship leader. Many pastors give little or no time in planning worship services. Worship planning can enrich the worship service and make it more appealing.

What can you do to plan for worship?

1. Recognize that the sermon is only one part of the total worship experience.

2. Seek to be led by the Holy Spirit as you do worship planning.

3. Develop a theme for the worship service. Scripture, sermon,

and musical selections all can support the chosen theme.

4. Include certain "givens" in your worship planning: hymns, Scripture readings, special music, prayers, testimonies, offering, sermon, greeting, announcements (though this list is not intended to be a complete list).

5. Use whatever resources are available: soloist, duet, drama, choir, testimony by someone in whose life God is working.

6. Emphasize the basic elements of worship: adoration and praise, introspection and confession, celebration and thanksgiving, proclamation and witness, dedication and commitment:

7. Plan ahead for congregational worship. Some services will need to be planned far in advance (especially seasonal services such as Christmas and Easter).

8. Consider the possibilities for worship on special occasions. These include:

New Year's Eve
Baptist Men's Day
Race Relations Sunday
Easter
Cooperative Program Sunday
Life Commitment Month
Mother's Day
Father's Day
Memorial Day
Religious Liberty Sunday
Independence Day
Labor Day
Single Adult Day
Senior Adult Day
Graduation Day
Children's Day
Covenant Sunday
Thanksgiving
Advent Sundays
Foreign Missions Day
Christmas
Student Night at Christmas
Lord's Supper
Baptism
Weddings
Funerals
Church anniversary or homecoming

Stewardship emphases
Deacon ordination
Pastor Appreciation Day
Worker Recognition Day
Recognition of public servants
High Attendance Sunday
Quarterly Hymn Sing
Parent-child dedication service
New member recognition
9. Consider worship services for special weeks:
WMU Focus Week
January Bible Study
Week of Prayer for Home Missions
Week of Prayer for Foreign Missions
Youth Week
Revivals
Baptist Doctrine Week
Christian Home Emphasis
Vacation Bible School
Church Music Week
State missions emphasis
Sunday School Preparation Week
Royal Ambassador Week

Using a Printed Worship Bulletin

I feel strongly, that if at all possible, some type of printed material should be provided to enhance congregational worship. The printed materials should give evidence of planning and involvement of the congregation.

Names of persons with responsibilities during the worship service should be printed. Sermon titles, Scripture selections, and hymn numbers should be listed. Printing the names of persons who will make announcements, pray, or sing shows good planning and gives evidence of a shared ministry.

Some quality standards for worship bulletins include:
• The bulletin should identify the church.
• The bulletin should serve as a guide for worship.
• The bulletin should list the names of worship leaders.
• The bulletin should be attractive.
• The bulletin should be read easily.
• The bulletin should identify musical selections.
• The bulletin should be typed correctly with no mispelled words.

You may order (Baptist Bulletin Service) tasteful, colorful, attractive bulletins from the Baptist Sunday School Board. They are priced at a low cost. The front of these bulletins shows an appropriate scene in full color. The inside of the bulletin is blank so you can print your orders of worship and announcements. The back page of these bulletins contains a timely missions message.

Some Ideas We Have Tried

Here are some things we have done to make worship alive, dynamic, vibrant, and meaningful for our people.

Worship committee.—Our church uses a worship committee that assists the pastor and music director in planning worship services. If this approach is not feasible for your church at least seek input from your people on a regular basis. Ask trusted individuals to help you evaluate the worship services in your church and to offer suggestions for improvement.

Congregational involvement.—Our members read Scripture, make announcements, sing special music, play musical instruments, give dramatic readings, and numerous other things. In our church, worship is not a spectator sport.

As pastor, I don't make a grand entrance into the service as if I was a prima donna. As a matter of fact, I stroll up and down the aisles and greet people prior to the service. Sometimes I will even take a seat beside a church member and just visit with him or her for a few minutes prior to the service.

Fall Harvest Festival.—This event is one of the most exciting of the year. We erect a tent on our property. The tent itself publicizes the event as well as the church. We have a special worship service each night of the week. We invite guest musicians to participate in our services. The major thrust of these services is on music. I conclude each of the services with a ten-minute Scripture challenge.

Meaningful celebrations of the ordinances.—I refuse to "tack on" baptism and the Lord's Supper to the end of a service. I make the celebration of these two ordinances central in our worship. I give these ordinances a service of their own.

Children's sermons.—A message just for the children in our church helps our boys and girls feel they are a part of the church, too. Sometimes, our adults get more out of the children's sermon than do the children.

We also have what our church calls "kaleidoscope" for preschoolers ages four and five. They are dismissed during the offering time for planned activities, lessons, and refreshments. This is not a babysitting event, but a learning experience.

Do not underestimate the important place of worship in the lives of your people and in the life of your church. Meaningful worship services give vitality to that which the people of God are about.

---

[1]W. T. Conner, *The Gospel of Redemption* (Nashville: Broadman Press, 1945), 277-78.
[2]Gary Farley, *Baptist Program,* April 1988, 10.

Resources

Aldridge, Marion D. *The Pastor's Guidebook: a Manual for Worship.* Nashville: Broadman Press, 1984.

Anderson, William M. Jr. *Music in the Worship Experience.* Nashville: Convention Press, 1984.

Bailey, Robert W. *New Ways in Christian Worship.* Nashville: Broadman Press, 1981.

Barry, James C., author/compiler. *Preach the Word in Love and Power.* Nashville: Convention Press, 1986.

Barry, James C. and Jack Gulledge, compilers/editors. *Ideas for Effective Worship Services.* Nashville: Convention Press, 1977.

Barry, James C. and Jack Gulledge, compilers/editors. *Sermons and Services for Special Days.* Nashville: Convention Press, 1979.

Barry, James C. and Fred Kelley. *How to Lead a Congregation to Be the People of God.* Nashville: Convention Press, 1986.

The Church Musician, Church Literature Dated Form.

Fish, Roy J. *Giving a Good Invitation.* Nashville: Broadman, 1974.

Fowler, J. B., Jr. *Illustrated Sermon Outlines.* Nashville: Broadman, 1987.

Hawkins, Frank. *The Church at Prayer.* Nashville: Broadman Press, 1986.

Hooper, William L. *Ministry and Musicians.* Nashville: Broadman Press, 1986.

Proclaim, Church Literature Dated Form.

Segler, Franklin M. *Christian Worship: Its Theology and Practice.* Nashville: Broadman Press, 1967.

Order church bulletins from Baptist Bulletin Service by calling 1-800-458-BSSB.

CHAPTER 7

Deacons: Serving as Partners in Ministry

Robert Sheffield

Robert Sheffield is consultant for deacon ministry, Church Administration Department, Baptist Sunday School Board.

I still can see the frustration on the face of that single-staff church pastor. He had shared with our group about his many responsibilities. These responsibilities even included the custodial work at the church. As this pastor spoke, two facts became obvious to me: (1) This pastor did not know how to involve other church members in the work of the church. (2) The deacons in his church did not understand their role.

The deacons in a single-staff church, as partners with the pastor, help enable the church to fulfill its mission. When deacons do not understand their role, or if the pastor and deacons cannot work together, the church fails to achieve its mission.

What Is a Deacon's Role?

Many deacons in single-staff churches have based their ministry role on traditions or cultural expectations rather than on Bible teachings. Of primary concern is who the deacon is as a Christian person. What we do flows out of who we are. A deacon's effectiveness often depends on how he sees himself and his role. Biblically, the word *deacon* means "servant." Sometimes the word is translated *minister*. Deacons, then, are servants who minister within the life of the church.

Christlike character qualities should mark the deacon/servant/minister: humility, unselfishness, kindness, generosity, love, commitment, faithfulness, patience, maturity, sensitivity, forgiving, willing, and a spirit of sacrifice. The quality of a deacon's servant ministry will depend on how well the deacon has cultivated these qualities in his life. Deacons can operate as a "board" without cultivating these qualities. But seldom will deacons carry out the role of ministering servants if these Christlike qualities are not evident in deacons' lives.

What can deacons do to cultivate these character qualities? Consider two actions. First, deacons must make a commitment to the ministering-servant role. Too often, deacons have committed themselves to a "board" or "church managers" concept of deacon work. This mistake usually results from viewing the church as a business or as an organization rather than as a spiritual organism.

In a single-staff church, the tension between a ministering-servants role and a managing, board of deacons concept can be especially strong.

Second, deacons must seek to grow spiritually. This step requires constant reliance on the leadership of the Holy Spirit. If a deacon's relationship with Jesus is not a quality relationship, then the deacon's relationship with the church will be lacking, too.

How Should Deacons Work With a Pastor?

Crucial to the health of a single-staff church is the relationship between deacons and the pastor. Without a staff, the pastor often finds the burdens of pastoring are more than he can bear. This dilemma is heightened for bivocational, single-staff pastors.

Pastors and deacons need not be competitors. Pastor and deacons must be a team of servants/ministers. To be sure, the pastor is leader of this team, but not a "boss" or "dictator."

"A team relationship between pastors and deacons develops

when it is recognized that in Christ's church there are no 'solo performers.' The need for tempermental pastors and tempermental deacons to do their work solo is out of step with the team concept. Like the hand needs the fingers to be the hand, we as pastors and deacons need one another to be a team." [1]

Deacons must not consider themselves as the pastor's supervisor or as the pastor's assistants. Nor can the pastor take the position of being the deacons' authority figure.

What actions can pastor and deacons take to build a team relationship? First, the pastor must affirm the deacons as individuals needed to help the church accomplish its mission. The pastor has a ministry role in the church. The deacons have their ministry role, too. The pastor alone does not have all the spiritual gifts needed for the church to be effective.

Second, the pastor can equip and train the deacons to use their gifts for ministry. Training in ministry skills enables deacons to be competent and confident in ministry. When deacons receive regular training they more readily accept their role as ministry partners with the pastor. Deacons need training in visitation skills, counseling skills, hospital and nursing home visitation, and witnessing, just to name a few areas. When deacons are trained for ministry, the pastor can feel better about sharing ministry with the deacons.

Third, the deacons must accept and enable the pastor in his role as leader of leaders. In some single-staff churches, the congregation has expected the deacons (or a certain deacon) to assume the leadership role. In such instances, the deacons might need to become less visible or less vocal and encourage the congregation to look to the pastor as leader. An example would be an older, wise deacon who encourages the congregation to regard their young pastor as a leader.

Fourth, deacons must help shoulder the church's ministry load. This step means the deacons don't view the pastor as a hired hand on whose shoulder falls the total load for the church's ministry. The result is that deacons perceive themselves as partners in ministry with the pastor rather than perceive themselves as the pastor's supervisor.

Fifth, pastor and deacons can cultivate Christian friendship. I remember well the friendships I shared with deacons during my first single-staff pastorate. I was a young pastor in those days. In this church, several of the deacons initiated friendships with me. They were patient with me, encouraged me, and gave me advice.

I have learned that when deacons and the pastor are friends there usually is mutual respect, trust, and sensitivity among pastor and deacons. The pastor is not trying to change the deacons or the deacons trying to change the pastor.

Any deacon deserves to know his pastor cares about him as a Christian person. In most single-staff churches, the deacons have served faithfully for many years. They have seen numerous pastors come and go. The deacons' tenure gives stability to the congregation. The deacons have earned this position of trust with the congregation. The pastor should accept this situation rather than fight it.

What are the Tasks of Deacon Ministry?

The term *pastoral ministries* doesn't refer only to the work of the pastor. Pastor and deacons do the work of pastoral ministries. They are responsible for three primary tasks: (1) leading the church to accomplish its mission, (2) proclaiming the gospel to believers and unbelievers, and (3) caring for church members and other persons in the community. The way deacon ministry is organized should grow out of these three tasks.

Proclaiming the gospel to believers and unbelievers.—This task includes worship, witnessing, and missions. In the single-staff church deacons can assist in worship services in these ways:

- make announcements,
- pray,
- lead congregational singing,
- give testimonies,
- receive the offering,
- greet visitors,
- read Scripture,
- assist the pastor in baptism,
- serve the Lord's Supper,
- counsel persons responding to the invitation,
- help the pastor evaluate worship services, and
- preach when asked.

The deacons can make evangelistic and prospect visits, teach witnessing training classes, and participate in missions projects sponsored by the church.

Caring for church members and other persons in the community.—This task includes hospital visitation, crisis intervention, benevolence needs, shut-in visitation, and nurturing new church members.

One ministry of care to be performed by deacons is that of caring for the pastor's family, including their financial needs. The deacons can lead the church to pay the pastor an adequate salary.

An additional way deacons can care for the pastor is through an understanding of the pastor's life changes. Young pastors in their twenties are just beginning their ministries. Deacons can become guides and teachers during this stage of the pastor's life. Pastors in their thirties tend to be productive but often neglect their families. Deacons should encourage a pastor to spend time with his family. During the forties, most pastors find their humanity catches up with them. The stress of teenage children, aging parents, financial demands, and job discouragement take a heavy toll on the pastor. The fifties can become another period of productivity for pastors as most of them have the maturity and experience at this stage to make major contributions. The sixties become a time to plan for closure to an active ministry. In all of these life stages, deacons can provide the ministry of care.[2]

Leading the church to accomplish its mission.—The pastor is a leader. But deacons are leaders, too. Healthy churches have dreams for an effective ministry. Deacons can work with the pastor in helping the congregation to dream. Deacons can lead by serving as catalyst-leaders—encouraging the church to get on with its mission. As catalyst-leaders, deacons model commitment to church growth, stewardship, fellowship, and missions activities.

Many extraordinary events occur in the life of a church. During these times, the effective leadership of the deacons becomes even more critical. I want to point out two examples: (1) when the church is without a pastor and (2) when conflict occurs in the church.

During an interim period deacons provide leadership by seeing that congregational worship services continue, assisting church program leaders to function, and by encouraging the church to choose appropriate committees. During an interim period, deacons are not to "run" the church, but are to give the kind of leadership that ensures ongoing church programs and ministries. Especially is this deacon leadership role crucial if the church does not have an active Church Council.

When the church is pastorless, a pastor-search committee must be formed, supply preachers must be enlisted, and the search for a pastor must be conducted. The deacons can assist the church in carrying out these tasks.

Since fellowship problems can arise easily during an interim period, deacons are needed to help maintain a sweet spirit in the church. One way deacons can help is by their maintaining an optimistic, hopeful attitude that finds its joy in the Lord.

When deacons need help with the various responsibilities that arise during an interim period, they often find the associational director of missions is an excellent resource person. He can give guidance as the church elects a pastor-search committee and begins its search for a new pastor. The state convention Pastoral Ministries program leader can be called on for help.

What about deacon leadership for managing conflicts? How deacons manage church conflict often determines whether a positive or negative experience will result from the conflict. Several suggestions might help.

First, at all times, deacons must be peacemakers. Second, on some occasions, deacons might need to confront persons in a Christlike way. At such times, hasty, thoughtless, or bossy actions can hinder the church rather than help the church. Third, any conflict should be approached in a spirit of prayer. Fourth, the goal of conflict management is to redeem persons, not destroy persons.

One of my co-workers once said, "A bulldog can whip a skunk, but it isn't worth it." I have had some experience trapping skunks. I know the stink caused sometimes isn't worth the effort. Stirring up a stink never is the best way to solve church conflicts.

How Can Deacon Ministry be Organized?
In most single-staff churches, deacon ministry can be organized simply. This statement does not mean deacon ministry has to be organized in a sloppy way. Remember the three tasks of deacon ministry I mentioned earlier? They are: (1) proclaiming the gospel to believers and unbelievers, (2) caring for the church's members and other persons in the community, and (3) leading the church to accomplish its mission. The approach taken to organize the church's deacon ministry must take these three tasks into account.

Here is a suggested process for organizing deacon ministry in the single-staff church. First, list areas of need in each of the three task areas. What are some needs in the areas of proclamation, care, and leadership?

Second, once needs are identified, prioritize the needs. Which ones seem to be most important?

Third, ask, How can the deacons of our church help meet these needs we have prioritized. What actions could the deacons take? What kind of deacon ministries could be developed to meet these needs?

Fourth, establish some goals arising from the list of prioritized needs. The entire deacon body should be allowed to give input to this listing of goals.

Fifth, develop an action plan for each goal.

Sixth, assign responsibility for carrying out these action plans. If the church has a large deacon body, several committees of deacons could be assigned these action plans.

Seventh, make progress reports at deacons' meetings throughout the year. Don't forget to make several progress reports to the church, too.

Eighth, at the end of the year, evaluate progress made, corrective actions needed, or changes needed, or better approaches that could be taken to accomplish the goals that were set.

Only a simple organizational structure is needed to carry out these actions: a deacon body chairperson, an associate chairperson, and a recording secretary. If the deacon body is large enough, and if there is a need, several deacon committees could be selected. For example, the deacons could elect a proclamation committee, care committee, and a leadership committee.

In churches where the Deacon Family Ministry Plan is used, one person should be chosen as the Deacon Family Ministry associate. Where there are enough deacons, one deacon can be asked to oversee deacon training activities.

What are Some Ways to Train Deacons for Ministry?

Trained deacons have more confidence for ministry. And having trained deacons inspires the congregation's confidence in the deacons. Training cannot be forced on deacons. Each deacon must admit his need for training and take steps to receive it.

The Deacon Ministry Diploma plans could become one avenue for training. By reading the several books that are part of the diploma plans, deacons are made aware of their role as ministering servants. Information about the diploma plans can be obtained by writing to the Church Study Course, 127 Ninth Avenue, North, Nashville, TN 37234.

A second avenue for training are the numerous associational and state deacon conferences and retreats. The associational Pastoral Ministries director will know of dates and locations for these events.

The Church Administration Department sponsors a third avenue for training: national deacon ministry conferences at Ridgecrest and Glorieta Baptist Conference Centers. Additionally, the Church Administration Department sponsors several regional deacon ministry conferences during the year.

A fourth training avenue are the monthly video messages broadcast on the Baptist Telecommunications Network (BTN). Each month, a fifteen-minute video message is aired through the program, "Equipping Deacons as Servant Leaders." Information about subscribing to BTN can be obtained by writing to BTN, 127 Ninth Avenue, North, Nashville, TN 37234.

A Fifth training avenue is a church-sponsored pastor-deacons-spouses retreat. A retreat is an excellent fellowship-building event.

Sixth, monthly deacons' meetings can include time set aside for training. This training time needs to focus on ministry skills. Perhaps twenty to thirty minutes of the deacons' meeting could be used for training purposes. The pastor could lead this training time, or the training period could be led by a deacon or by an outside resource person. The BTN video message series, "Equipping Deacons as Servant Leaders" could be used effectively for training times during monthly deacons' meetings.

An eighth resource is *The Deacon,* a quarterly magazine. Order this periodical from the Baptist Sunday School Board, 1-800-458-BSSB.

A crucial area that needs to be studied once every few years is the church's deacon election procedure. If the church's election procedure does not promote the election of biblically qualified deacon ministers who are committed to a ministry approach to deacon work, the church's election procedures should be changed.

Any election procedure changes should be made as a result of church vote during business meeting session. One caution in deciding which kind of election procedure to use is to use a procedure that doesn't call for a run-off vote. Ideally, the church's election procedure reflects God's will in selecting individuals who have servants' hearts rather than those persons who seek position, power, or prominence.

Some churches find helpful using a special committee of the church to nominate qualified deacon candidates. No matter which deacon election process is used, the election should not infer that the deacons are a self-perpetuating group. The deacons should have a clear understanding that they have been chosen by congregational vote, through the Lord's leadership, and that they are responsible to the Lord and to the church.

How Much Should Deacons in a Single-Staff Church Be Expected to Do?

Deacons in a single-staff church do run the risk of ministry burn-out. I remember a deacon and his spouse who visited the church I pastored. For many years, this man had served faithfully as a deacon in a single-staff church. When I asked for the reason they were visiting our church, I learned this man felt he had been caught in a "church activity" trap. This man not only served that single-staff church as a faithful deacon but he also served in numerous other roles. He was burned out on church work. He said, "If I join this church (the church I pastored), I don't want to do anything for a year. I need time to regather my energy, spiritually and physically."

The answer to this kind of dilemma rests partly with the church and partly with the deacon. The congregation must realize that if it wants deacons who minister, then those deacons can't be asked to serve in numerous other church jobs. I have known deacons who served as Sunday School director, deacon chairperson, adult choir member, and committee member, all at the same time.

A pastor can be a big help at this point of concern. A pastor who accepts his equipping/training responsibility seriously, will continually be training other persons to assume leadership roles in the church. When trained/equipped persons are available, the church's ministry can be shared.

In this chapter I have tried to show that an effective deacon ministry is a partnership between the pastor, the deacons, and the congregation. The road to an effective deacon ministry in a single-staff church might be steep at times. It might take an occasional curve. But, when the leadership of the Holy Spirit is sought, this road will lead to a powerful, joyful, and biblical deacon ministry.

---

[1]Howard B. Foshee, *Now That You're A Deacon* (Nashville: Broadman Press, 1975), 24.

[2]David C. George, "Helping Your Pastor Be Human," *The Deacon,* October 1984, 8.

98

Resources

Carter, Homer D. *Equipping Deacons in Caring Skills.* Nashville: Convention Press, 1980.

The Deacon, Church Literature Dated Form.

Deweese, Charles. *The Emerging Role of the Deacon.* Nashville: Broadman Press, 1980.

Sheffield, Robert. *The Ministry of Baptist Deacons.* Nashville: Convention Press, 1989.

Sheffield, Bob. *Deacon Ministry Planning Guide.* Nashville: Convention Press, 1989.

Sheffield, Bob. *Equipping Deacons in Caring Skills, Volume II.* Nashville: Convention Press, 1989.

Webb, Henry, author/compiler. *Equipping Deacons as Partners in Ministry.* Nashville: Convention Press, 1985.

Webb, Henry, compiler. *Equipping Deacons in Church Growth Skills.* Nashville: Convention Press, 1982.

When Families Hurt, Deacons Can Help, Undated Materials Order Form.

White, James E. *Deacon Retreat Planning Guide.* Nashville: Convention Press, 1986.

White, James E. and Robert L. Sheffield. *Equipping Deacons to Confront Conflict.* Nashville: Convention Press, 1987.

CHAPTER 8

Stewardship: Supporting the Church's Ministry

Jim Rich

Jim Rich is stewardship director, Missouri Baptist Convention, Jefferson City, Missouri.

D. G. McCoury has identified the possible frustrations often faced by single-staff pastors. "How do you choose priorities in a single-staff church? How do you deal with sickness, bereavement, and/or personal needs of the congregation; prepare sermons; manage the organizations; check on programs; balance the budget? How can a pastor choose priorities when he has both immediate and ongoing needs?"[1]

Did D. G. say, "Balance the budget?" Many single-staff churches see no need for a budget. Some single-staff congregations even feel the pastor is wrong to mention money from the pulpit. On the opposite end are single-

staff congregations who face great financial needs. Both of these congregations (those who see no need for a budget and those who do not want the pastor mentioning money) face a similar challenge: stewardship development.

Many years ago, Gaines Dobbins, a great Southern Baptist educator, stated that Christians have two responsibilities that go together. Christians must be evangelists who bring people to a saving knowledge of Christ. Christians, he pointed out, must also be stewards who allow Jesus to be Lord of every area of their lives.[2] We don't have to be faithful stewards to be saved. But because we are saved we should be faithful stewards. Pastor, resist the temptation to neglect stewardship development. Guide the church in its stewardship program. Are you thinking, *How do I do this?* Let me offer some suggestions.

Step 1: Understand Stewardship

Stewardship is important in Christian living. Life is a sacred trust. Because God has given us the gift of life, we are accountable to God for what we do with life.

Christian stewardship is rooted in a personal relationship with God. Salvation in Christ frees us to channel our lives as Christian servants. What we do for God grows out of what God already has done for us. To be a steward is to be a manager of all God has given us.

The following stewardship concepts will help Christians grow in their faith and in their practice of stewardship. Teach and preach these truths often.

• God is the creator of all things (Col. 1:16-17).
• To humans has been entrusted the responsibility to be managers of what God has given us. (Luke 12:37-48).
• Stewardship is a life-style in which God has priority (Matt. 6:33).
• Material things should be used for God's glory and for persons' good (1 John 3:17).
• Christian giving is a grace to be developed (2 Cor. 8:7).
• The purpose and mission of the church are related closely to stewardship (Acts 2:42-47).
• A growing commitment to Christ is the key to faithful stewardship (2 Cor. 8:5).[3]

Stewardship involves the individual.—The Christian steward (1) affirms God's ownership of all things, (2) accepts his accountability to God, and (3) actively manages God's entrusted gifts. The

Christian pursues God's purpose in working and earning, spending and saving, and giving and planning for the future. Each believer must be taught and guided in his or her management of material things.

The church is a teacher of stewardship.—The church must live under the lordship of Jesus. The church should manage wisely its financial and human resources. The church must seek to use its monies in a way that reflects a commitment to God's great purposes. The church is important to the individual Christian because it is through the church that the Christian will channel his or her stewardship.

Step 2: The Pastor Assumes His Role
The pastor's personal example of and attitude about stewardship usually becomes a model for church members. What can a pastor do to enhance his personal example and attitude?

1. *He can grow in the grace of his personal giving.*—The pastor, along with other church members, can develop a habit of sacrificial giving in support of the church's ministries.

2. *He can express joy for Christians who grow in their stewardship.*—Christians who develop as stewards are becoming what God wants them to be in the area of management of possessions.

3. *He can identify himself with the stewardship program of the church.*—The pastor does this by preaching and teaching on stewardship and by praying for a high quality of stewardship development in the church. Most pastors who preach on stewardship do so at budget time. Why not preach on stewardship at times when the church is not developing its annual budget?

4. *He can lead the church's stewardship ministry.*—A small Baptist congregation in Rifle, Colorado, met in a two-bedroom house away from the town's flow of traffic. About twenty people attended the church's Sunday School. The pastor and his family lived in the basement of the church building (the two-bedroom house). This pastor decided that stewardship development was an absolute must for his congregation.

He began his stewardship development strategy during a morning worship service by preaching on the biblical basis of stewardship. He and his family set an example in their personal giving. He arranged for stewardship seminars (the most successful was a Christian money-management conference) to be taught to the congregation.

The congregation voted to use a simple budget program (the Great Challenge Budget Program). With this program, members determined the church's ministry needs and then made personal giving commitments to support the church's ministries.

A ministry need identified by the congregation was the need for a church building. By using a consultant-led capital fund raising campaign, eight families made several-year giving commitments that totaled more than $160,000. The church bought another building along a busy highway and turned that building into a church meetinghouse. The old, two-bedroom house was remodeled as a home for the pastor's family. The progress of this church was made possible because its pastor led the church in its stewardship ministry.

Step 3: Elect a Stewardship Committee
A pastor cannot be the only stewardship spokesperson in the church. Using a committee to help with the church's stewardship development is not a new idea. Experience has taught we Baptists that by using committees we enable people to use their spiritual gifts in the church's work, we encourage their commitment to the church's ministry, and we involve more people in Kingdom work.

Does your church presently have a budget committee? a stewardship committee? no committee at all? Start where you are. If you have no committee at all, educate the people about Christian stewardship. Teach the people the values to be gained from a planned emphasis on stewardship development. Then lead the church to elect a stewardship committee.

Perhaps your church already has a budget or finance committee. Usually this committee has one main focus: finances or making a church budget. Focusing on finances and budgets is fine, but biblical stewardship is much more than budgets. A stewardship committee can plan yearlong strategies for educating your people about stewardship. This committee can become an advocate for your church's financial support of missions. By using a stewardship committee, more people in your church will become involved in stewardship development.

A stewardship committee should address at least four areas of stewardship work:

1. *Stewardship education.*—The committee will develop and recommend to the church programs and activities that teach biblical stewardship.

2. *Missions support.*—Church members must be taught to support missions work financially. As the stewardship committee addresses this area of stewardship development, the committee will become an advocate for Cooperative Program giving.

3. *Budget.*—The committee will plan a budget to recommend to the church. After the budget is approved by the church, the stewardship committee then assumes responsibility for promoting and encouraging church members' financial support of the budget.

4. *Accounting.*—The stewardship committee will take steps to ensure that sound procedures for collecting, counting, safeguarding, and disbursing funds are used.

If your church has a small membership, as few as three people could do the work of the stewardship committee. One person could be assigned the stewardship education responsibilities, one person the missions support responsibilities, one person the accounting, and all three members the development of the budget.

If your church presently uses only a budget or a budget-finance committee, why not consider enlarging the responsibilites of this committee to include responsibility for stewardship education, missions support, and accounting.

Step 4: Plan for a Year at a Time
Your church's responsibility for teaching members stewardship is too large a task to be limited to only one brief emphasis each year. What is needed is a yearlong program of stewardship education. Again, the members of the stewardship committee can help with planning for stewardship education activities. But, even if your church is opposed to the idea of enlarging the responsibilities of the old budget-finance committee, don't fail to provide stewardship education emphases all year long.

Start by planning a stewardship calendar that covers each aspect of Christian stewardship: earning, spending, giving, and planning for the future. If your church uses a Church Council, the chairperson of the stewardship committee should serve on the Church Council. By using this approach, you are assured that stewardship education activities and events are placed on the church's calendar.

Some stewardship activities are built into the denominational calendar, already. For example, January is "Make Your Will Month." The months of March, April, September, October, and December lend themselves to support of missions emphases.

Step 5: Develop, Adopt, and Promote a Budget

Maybe your church never has used a budget and you are wondering, *What is a budget anyway?* Technically, a budget is a written plan for allocating the church's financial resources toward the church's ministry goals. A budget declares the church's intentions. Church members should be able to read the budget and then know what the church plans to accomplish during the year.

Did you know that one-third of our Southern Baptist churches do not project their ministries through a written budget? This fact is tragic! Of course, these churches know some financial needs can be anticipated: missions giving, salaries, building payments, and educational supplies. Other bills are paid as they are received. New purchases are approved as the needs are recognized. What is wrong with this approach is: (1) there is no intentional purpose behind the use of the church's money and (2) often various organizations or groups within the church have separate funds for their work.

1. *Begin by electing a budget planning committee.*—If the church already has a budget or a stewardship committee, this group will be the one to develop and recommend a budget. If your church has neither of these committees, then your church will need to elect a special group to develop and recommend a budget.

2. *Determine a budgeting process.*—Two methods are the most often used by our churches: line-item budgeting and church ministry budgeting.

The line-item approach allocates money for each item when there is an expected expenditure. Input from committees and organizations is welcomed, but usually, dollars are requested without any indication of the ministries to be performed by those committees or organizations. Heavy reliance is placed on past expenditures, and activities are maintained on a more or less constant level. The various line items usually are:
- Missions
- Personnel
- Education
- Special ministries
- Building

Beneath each of these section headings the committee will list the related item and the money allocated.

The church ministry budgeting approach is one whereby the church plans its spending around the ministries it wants to do during the coming year. Rather than focusing attention on a list of expense items for which funds are to be raised, the church ministry approach is concerned with what the church wants to accomplish. The budget would be divided into categories related to the church's objectives and mission. This process can be used by a church of forty members or a church of five thousand members. The church ministry approach to budgeting begins by asking these questions (This may come as a recommendation from the Church Council, or in a smaller membership church that usually serves as a "committee of the whole," it can be done in a regular or special meeting.):

- What ministries should our church be engaged in next year?
- How much will these ministries cost?
- Is there a better way to get the job done?

Ministry proposals are the most crucial step. The budget or stewardship committee would ask each committee and organization to list its ministry plans for the year and the estimated cost of each ministry plan. These are developed into a budget that reflects church ministries rather than line-item expenses.

Sample ministry areas are:
- Our world mission ministries
- Our pastoral ministries
- Our educational ministries
- Our music ministries
- Our supportive ministries
- Our building and grounds ministries

The church ministry approach to budgeting has no staff salary section. The salaries of the pastor and part-time persons would appear in the budget section which alludes to their ministries. Benefits and related expenses for these persons would appear in the supportive ministry section.

Some churches of smaller memberships have used successfully still a third approach to budgeting. It is called "Simplified Budgeting for Ministries." With this approach, the entire congregation is assembled to begin the development of the budget. The congregation will deal with four questions in this meeting:
- What ministries should our church do next year?
- Why should we do these ministries?
- How shall we do these ministries?
- How much will these ministries cost and are we willing to

commit the money to them?

In some churches, this work can be done in one session. The information from this congregational meeting is given to the budget or stewardship committee with the request that, as much as possible, the congregation's dreams be reflected in the proposed budget submitted to the church for approval.

Still another approach to developing the budget is to have a churchwide dinner. At this dinner, members of the congregation are asked to submit at least five ministry priorities they feel the church should address for the coming year. These are collected, tabulated, and then become the basis for ministry proposals that go into the completed budget.

3. *Prepare the budget.*—Having gathered ideas and information from people, the assigned committee recommends a budget. This committee will consider these areas:
- total dollar amounts requested,
- advisable dollar amounts to be requested,
- alternative dollar amounts,
- how funds should be allocated according to the importance of the ministry, and
the best way for listing the item in the budget.

4. *Present the budget.*—Prepare the budget copy in a way that shows clearly the various church programs or ministries. Do all you can to help church members translate listed budget items into ministries. Why? So that ministries and offerings become linked together.

Encourage members to participate in a discussion of the budget. You can encourage members to discuss the budget by using one of these approaches.
- Direct mail. Mail a copy of the budget to members' homes prior to the presentation meeting.
- Fellowship dinner. Discuss the budget at a pot-luck supper.
- Use audiovisuals. Have a creative person in the church develop a slide or video presentation of the budget.
- Panel. The members of the budget committee would make up a panel. To each member of the budget would be assigned a section of the budget to be presented. The panel sits in front of the congregation and answers questions asked by church members.
- Visitation. A copy of the budget is delivered personally to homes of the church family. The visitor will deal with questions and concerns about the budget and will encourage support of

the budget.

5. *Promote the budget.*—Promotion of the budget is simply telling the church's story to every member. Ways to promote the budget include sermons, testimonies, and commitment cards.

Step 6: Emphasize Missions
At the center of your church should be ministries which show your congregation has a heart for missions. A portion of your printed budget will show financial support for certain missions causes. Educate your people about these areas. The more information people have, the more willing they are to lend financial support.

Missions support needs a strong advocate in your church. People tend to support what they know and what they have been told about. Provide continuous information about missions work all year long.

The month of October is the month on the denominational calendar given to provide information about and encourage support of the Cooperative Program. Associational Missions Emphasis Week is scheduled in May. Easter and Christmas are the time to promote the two national offerings for home and foreign missions.

Step 7: Use Available Resources
Become familiar with the resources listed at the end of this chapter. In addition to this list, you may obtain a catalog filled with helpful materials for stewardship development. For a copy of this catalog write to SBC Stewardship Services, 601 Commerce St., Nashville, TN.

---

[1]D. G. McCoury, "The Single-Staff Church: Meeting the Demands." *The Quarterly Review,* October-December 1987, 12.

[2]Gaines S. Dobbins, *The Churchbook* (Nashville: Broadman Press, 1951), 170.

[3]Ernest D. Standerfer and Lee E. Davis, *Christian Stewardship in Action* (Nashville: Convention Press, 1983), 15.

Resources

Baker, Robert A. and Daniel Vestal. *Pulling Together!* Nashville: Broadman Press, 1987.

Bisagno, John R. *The Power of Positive Giving.* Nashville: Broadman Press, 1988.

Carter, James E. *A Sourcebook of Stewardship Sermons.* Nashville: Broadman Press, 1972.

Church Administration, Church Literature Dated Form.

The Church Stewardship Committee, Church Materials Order Form.

Davis, Lee E. *Choose the Best.* Nashville: Convention Press, 1985.

Davis, Lee E. and Ernest D. Standerfer. *Christian Stewardship in Action.* Nashville: Convention Press, 1983.

Fagan, A. R. *What the Bible Says About Stewardship.* Nashville: Convention Press, 1976.

Hendricks, William L., editor. *Resource Unlimited.* Nashville: Stewardship Commission of the Southern Baptist Convention, 1972.

Ray, Cecil and Susan Ray. *Cooperation: the Baptist Way to a Lost World.* Nashville: Stewardship Commission of the Southern Baptist Convention, 1985.

Ray, Cecil. *Living the Responsible Life.* Nashville: Convention Press, 1974.

The Stewardship Ministry Plan Book. Order from Stewardship Commission, 127 Ninth Avenue, North, Nashville, TN 37234.

Preaching Helps on Stewardship. Order from Stewardship Commission, 127 Ninth Avenue, North, Nashville, TN 37234.

Church Ministry Budgeting. Order from Stewardship Commission, 127 Ninth Avenue, North, Nashville, TN 37234.

◆ **CHAPTER 9** ◆

Guidelines
for the Guide

D. G. McCoury

D. G. McCoury is consultant for pastoral ministries, single-staff church, and the associational program of Pastoral Ministries, Church Administration Department, Baptist Sunday School Board.

How would you describe your ministry as a single-staff church leader? Ministry is *fulfilling* when you know Christ is working in your life. Ministry is *effective* when it is motivated by the Holy Spirit and conducted according to spiritual gifts. Ministry is *comprehensive* when the entire congregation is involved in the church's work. Ministry is *powerful* when church members are bound by a sweet fellowship. And, ministry is *successful* when the congregation is reaching the goals they have set under Christ's lordship.

Is this kind of ministry only a dream? No. To guide your church toward this reality, practice the suggestions men-

tioned in the chapters you have just read.
 • Understand the nature and mission of the church.
 • Develop and work with the leadership team the church has selected.
 • Help the church, through this leadership team, to study biblical church growth, church needs, and ministry resources. Then, establish spiritual directions (ministry plans).
 • Organize and use the various programs whose assigned tasks (see page 25) will provide "handles" to accomplish your ministry plans.
 • Rejoice, celebrate, and affirm the church when goals are reached.

For several years, I served the Colorado Baptist Convention as its Associate Executive Director and Church Administration/Pastoral Ministries Director. In these positions, I had the privilege of being the field supervisor for several pastors who were working toward a Doctor of Ministry degree through Southwestern Baptist Theological Seminary. Part of the requirements for this degree included the development of a ministry project. I noticed these pastors wanted to develop exotic, lavish ministry projects. None of the pastors were inclined toward doing the basics, the fundamentals as we have presented them in this book.

I was, however, able to convince a Denver mission pastor to start with the basics and to see if these basics would assist his church to have an effective ministry.

Never underestimate the influence of your church's founding pastor. Sometimes, this influence can be just as powerful in an older church that has lost, or never discovered, its identity. In such a situation, the pastor (or an influential member) has incredible influence in terms of shaping the congregation's beliefs, administrative procedures, polity, and future. The tone of ministry and the style of leadership displayed determine the following matters:
 • What type of church eventually will emerge;
 • Who will be attracted to it;
 • What the church will believe;
 • Which educational materials the church will use;
 • The church's missions commitment as expressed through Cooperative Program giving; and
 • The growth potential of the church.

The founding pastor really does help create the congregational culture. Church leaders should recognize their responsibility to build ministry characteristics into the church that reflect Southern Baptist heritage, rather than the pet ideas of the founding pastor. Early church decisions do become precedents. These early decisions must be consistent with the church's statement of purpose. Most important is that these early decisions reflect biblical doctrine.

With these thoughts in mind, I want to share a testimony from the doctor of ministry student I mentioned in earlier paragraphs (This is the student whom I urged to begin with the basics.) Let's call this pastor Jerry.

A Testimony

On July 28, 1981, our family arrived in Denver, Colorado, to begin the most exciting days we have ever known in ministry. I had been called as pastor of a mission congregation in Aurora, Colorado, a suburb located on the eastern side of the Denver metropolitan area. Foremost in my mind was the desire to see the mission congregation grow. I wanted to see it blossom into a strong self-governing, self-supporting, self-propagating church.

The congregation was small—less than thirty members. They had struggled for three years, were tired and discouraged, but determined. The church's services were conducted in an elementary school building on Sunday mornings, a Lutheran church on Sunday evenings, and in our home on Wednesday nights.

I came to the church with three basic convictions about growing a church. First, growth would require total congregational involvement. Second, the entire congregation would have to share a common vision of what they could become. And, third, the vision would be meaningless if we did not plan ways to make the vision a reality.

So, from the beginning, I set out to plant these ideas into the hearts of the people. We planned a churchwide retreat for November 1981. Our purpose was to plan ways to accomplish our dream. I wanted to involve as many church members as possible. Sixteen of the twenty-one adults in our church attended the retreat. Our state convention's Pastoral Ministries director taught us some basic principles of church administration.

During the retreat, we studied church growth and church planning. We dreamed, fellowshiped, and planned together. We left the retreat convinced that by trusting God and one another we could grow.

In the months that followed, our church grew. We soon realized that numerical growth wasn't the only kind of growth we needed. Organizational growth and the development of believers had to parallel numerical growth. Our church decided that we must broaden our leadership base so we could minister to the needs of our congregation.

The fruit of our growth was evident. The church elected a building committee. Nineteen months of hard work passed before we ever broke ground. Then, in May 1982, a steering committee was elected to prepare us to constitute as a church. This committee guided our church, during an eighteen month period, to develop a church constitution and by-laws, a deacon's manual, and a church policy manual.

In April 1982, the church elected a committee on committees. This group operated for the next three years with one main guideline—spread the responsibilities for leadership throughout the entire church membership. This approach worked. People who never had served were asked to serve. Some of these persons weren't strong Christians, but we trained them and equipped them for their jobs.

Other essential committees were formed. In September 1982, the chairpersons of these committees, along with our Church Council members, gathered for a second planning retreat. Once again, we dreamed and planned. The committee chairpersons became a part of our Church Council. We met monthly to coordinate the church's work. We made some mistakes. But, as time passed, we began to see our dream become reality.

In April 1983, we were formally constituted as a church with more than one hundred active members. In June 1983, we broke ground for our building. Our church's members gave hundreds of hours of personal time in the construction of the building. In September 1983, we elected our first deacons. Two requirements had been established for our deacons: (1) Each deacon would commit himself to the Deacon Family Ministry Plan. And, (2) each deacon would complete the requirements for earning the Deacon Ministry Diploma through the Church Study Course Awards Program. Our first deacons served well and earned their diplomas.

In March 1984, we moved into our building. Much work remained to be done with the parking lot and landscaping. But, for the time being, we were in our own building. The people who lived in our community now could see a physical building that identified our congregation as the people of God.

In the meantime, we had seen numerous planning projects and programs. For example, in May 1984, we sponsored our first mission, which met in another part of an eastern Denver suburb. As we moved into 1985, we had grown from thirty members to 278 members. Our Sunday School enrollment was four hundred.

Observations about Guiding

I believe this testimony shows us five important leadership strategies you can practice.

1. Set up a long-term agenda (strategic planning) as well as a short-term agenda (day-to-day operations).

2. Put together a network of relationships (Church Council, committees, deacons).

3. Effectively guide that network of people (organizations) to implement both agendas.

4. Use a flexible, participative leadership style.

5. Administratively, be a generalist leader. The church's program directors are the specialist for their assigned programs. Work with these persons through the Church Council.

As a wise pastoral guide, Jerry used a participative style coupled with extensive delegation. Once a decision or plan was approved, Jerry relied on the church's leadership team and the assigned program to carry out actions needed. Jerry avoided what I consider to be *fatal errors* in pastoral leadership.

1. Refusing to accept personal accountability;

2. Failing to develop people;

3. Doing church without a mission statement owned by all;

4. Dreaming and making decisions alone;

5. Majoring only on numerical growth, while neglecting other kinds of growth;

6. Establishing programs before the church has adequate organization and sufficient resources—leaders, budget, space, and so forth;

7. Expecting individuals to assume responsibilities without guidelines, training, and needed resources;

8. Trying to lead every person in the same way;

9. Trying to manipulate people;

10. Involving and/or recognizing only a few people;

11. Concentrating on problems rather than on objectives;

12. Trying to control results rather than influencing the thinking of the people.

As Jerry took the initiative to guide the mission of thirty members to become a self-supporting church, the work the congregation did indicated the people understood their purpose. This congregation expressed key commitments including integrity, service, sensitivity, and leadership. The people were driven by biblical values and worked within adopted plans.

Guiding Questions

Jerry's leadership succeeded partly because he led the congregation to discover their mission and to make plans to accomplish that mission. Many single-staff churches just do not have a sense of purpose or direction. We can't assume our church has a sense of purpose simply because we have weekly worship services and one or two church programs.

I have observed that many single-staff churches are either in a "maintenance mode" or in a "rescue mode." These churches react rather than act. The church might talk about church growth, but no specific plans for growth are ever developed.

If a single-staff church pastor is to guide his church out of the wilderness of having no purpose, he must lead the church to ask these questions.

• Who are we as the people of God?

• Does our church have a well-defined mission statement (basic purpose, reason for being a church).

• Is the mission statement understood by everyone in the church? (I am convinced many church members show limited involvement because they do not know the purpose of their church, much less feel any ownership in the church's work.)

• What is the current mood of our congregation?

• What are our church's current goals, strategies, and plans.

• Are these goals, strategies, and plans stated clearly or merely implied?

• Are our goals and plans consistent with our stated mission?

• What general environmental factors (economic, sociocultural, political, and technological) are affecting us? (This question deals with community typology.)

• Which of these environmental factors are the most pressing now? Which ones will affect us most ten years from now?

• How is the church organization presently structured? Is it organized on the basis of people, program tasks, annual plans, leadership, finances, or some combination of these?

• Is the present organization consistent with current goals, strategies, and plans.

• In what ways does our organization compare to those of similar churches that are growing?

• What is the congregation's position on important issues facing the church (such as programs, polity, administrative procedures, use of resources, community needs, and leadership)?

• What are some short-term challenges facing this congregation?

• Does there need to be some fine tuning for us to achieve our

present goals?
- What alternatives are available to us?
- Do we need to emphasize stability, growth, retrenchment, or a combination of these strategies at the present time?
- Do we have the resources to do the job? Are these needed resources available?
- How well are we addressing the four areas of biblical growth: evangelism, discipleship, missions, administration?
- Do our members need instruction in the nature and work of a Southern Baptist church?

All of these questions are important, but we could summarize them this way.
1. Who are we (mission statement)?
2. What are our church and community needs (ministry)?
3. What does our church want to accomplish (goals)?
4. How are we going to get desired results (procedure)?
5. How will we define and assign responsibility (delegation)?
6. What standards and controls are needed (budgets, schedules, checkpoints, review meetings)?

Excellent help for dealing with these kinds of questions can be obtained by studying the resources listed at the end of this chapter.

Don't be overwhelmed by all these questions. I am not speaking about developing some big, impressive report for church adoption. The goal is simply to break out of a pattern in which the church merely goes in circles and to bring some intentional planning into the life of the church.

Leadership Defined
Remember that we give leadership by working with and through (influencing) individuals and groups to develop and accomplish goals that are in keeping with our church's mission. As you provide this kind of leadership, involve the whole church as best you can. People are motivated when they have a part in determining or reshaping their church's goals. You are the guide who must assist the church to discover its mission.

Directional Planning
After your church has dealt with the previously mentioned questions, the next step is to begin to do planning. Annual plans will help your members maintain their current commitments. Goals and plans need to be reexamined annually. Annual planning helps

us adjust priorities when needed. Annual planning enables us to concentrate time and money on things that really matter. Carefully laid, annual plans provide the structures for churches to see their mission through the eyes of faith.

Directional planning really involves several types of planning. *Annual planning* is what we want to do during the next year. *Regular planning* is the day-to-day planning we do to accomplish our annual plans. *Long-range planning* is what we want to do three to five years from now. Many single-staff churches are not ready for long-range planning because they haven't mastered annual planning. But, it's best to have annual plans that tie in with and support the church's long-range plans. Single-staff churches that average forty to sixty in weekly Sunday School attendance will probably do their planning through events or projects. (More will be said later about this approach.)

The planning cycle looks like this.

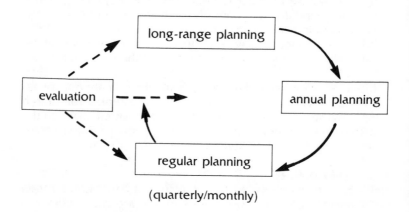

(quarterly/monthly)

Basic Annual Planning

Here is a basic outline for doing annual planning in a single-staff church.

1. *Organize or revive a Church Council.*—(In a smaller membership church, planning usually takes place through church business meeting decisions. Some single-staff churches will not be open to pastoral leadership for annual planning because these churches work off the rhythm of yearly events and projects.)

2. *Discover needs in the church and the community.*

• Some needs are obvious and need only to be listed.

- Briefly evaluate what was done last year and in previous years.
- Discover needs by listening to and observing the people.
- Study the church's Uniform Church Letter. It will reveal areas of need.
- Conduct a survey or use an evaluation instrument to let the people identify their perceived needs.
- See if the basic church programs are doing their assigned tasks. (See the task statements on page 26).
- Evaluate what your church is doing through the Church Study Course plan and which Church Study Course diplomas have been awarded during the past five years.
- Evaluate the need for an emphasis program to strengthen the work of your church's basic programs. (See the listing of emphasis programs on page 28).
- Talk with your associational director of missions concerning emphases in the association or state convention.
- Gather information from local agencies that can help you know about changes in the community.

3. *Determine priority needs.*—Probably, you will identify more needs than you can meet in one year, so some needs will need to be targeted for the long-range planning cycle.

4. *Establish goals for each priority need listed.*—Goal setting will give specific direction to your work. Goals should be

- challenging,
- attainable,
- measurable,
- stated clearly, and
- given a completion date.

As you set your goals, consider available resources. You might not have the needed resources to reach some goals. Present these goals to the church for adoption.

5. *Decide the kind of support or changes your basic programs need.*—Do you need to set a goal to start a new basic program? (See page 26 for a listing of basic church programs.) Or could you develop one of the emphasis programs or service programs (see listings on pages 28-29).

6. *Choose the events, activities, and projects you want to schedule for this year.*—These need to speak to the goals set earlier.

7. *Place these events and activities on the church's calendar.*—More will be said about calendaring.

8. *Report to the church and recommend the calendar of ac-*

tivities for adoption.

9. *Determine budget needs.*—Once you have planned your calendar of activities for the year, determine how much money you will need for all the various events and activities. Include monies for programs, mailings, materials, literature, personnel, child care, meals, and promotion.

10. *Present your list of budget needs to the budget planning group.*

11. *After the calendar and budget have been approved, each activity on the calendar needs to be planned.*—For some events you will need to plan far in advance. Regular planning meetings will take care of month-to-month events.

If you have done effective planning, you will have answered these basic questions: (1) What work needs to be done? (2) What actions are necessary to get the work done? (3) Who will do the work? (4) When will the work be done? And, (5) How will the work be done?

To put the final touch on your planning, evaluate your completed activities, programs, and events by asking these questions: (1) How well was the work done? (2) Did we reach our goal? (3) How can the work be done better next time? (4) Do we need to plan the same way again?

Basic Church Calendaring

I want to focus your attention on the steps needed to plan a calendar of activities for the year. When designing your calendar work with the Church Council.

1. Begin by entering all regular, ongoing activities. Examples would be Sunday School, Church Training, deacons' meetings, WMU meetings.

2. Enter special, all-church events on the calendar. Examples would be a revival, homecoming, Vacation Bible School.

3. Request dates for church program organization meetings, committee meetings, and projects from the various program directors and committee chairpersons.

4. Enter all dates submitted by programs and committees.

5. Enter associational, state, and SBC activities on the calendar.

6. Coordinate the various calendar dates:
   - Find conflicts in dates and evaluate weeks where there are too many events.
   - Eliminate these conflicts by rearranging dates.
   - Seek balance on the calendar.

7. Submit the completed calendar to the church for approval.

"Event/Project" Planning

If your church is a smaller membership church and is an established church, you might want to try what I call "event/project" planning. This approach works better in a church that doesn't respond well to a pastor who initiates planning and calendaring. These churches are not interested in ongoing, week-by-week programming that denominational boards and agencies promote. These congregations do their work with events or projects rather than with programs or annual planning.

If you are more in tune with "programmatic" congregations, you will have to adapt to the smaller membership church's event/project way of doing church. Here is an important leadership strategy for the pastor. He must stand in the middle of the church's history and understand why the church does things the way it does.

Never try to "kill" the church's annual events nor seek to turn or channel their energy into ongoing programs and plans if the members are not ready to do so. If you do, you will end up frustrated, ignored, or rejected for your efforts.

I like the following story as told by Gary Farley of our Home Mission Board.

Pastors at Burr's Branch often joked about the Holy Spirit only coming to that church during the second week in August. Wise pastors realized there was a logical reason for holding the revival at that time. The second cutting of hay was in, crops were laid by, and the people in this farming community had some free time.

Once, Harvey, the county court judge, complained about the cost of these revival meetings, questioning their usefulness. But the deacons—Pacey, Lefty, Gummy, and Jim—set him straight. As long as anyone could remember, and Burr's Branch was more than one hundred years old, revival was held the second week in August.

The revivals there took on elements of a homecoming or reunion. Family and former members who had moved away to Kansas City or St. Joseph planned to "be back home" during the second week of August. Grandparents insisted that their grandchildren come for a visit during the second week in August. No church within fifteen miles planned a competing event during the second week in August. Rather, they provided the special music for the revival at least one night. And to the minds of most people, nothing could compare to the dinner on the grounds on the final

Sunday of the revival meeting. Usually, a baptizing was part of the celebration of that Sunday afternoon.

In the weeks before the second week in August, the church house was painted, polished, and pampered. Harvey had the county crew grade the road, put some gravels in the parking lot, and cleaned out the ditches and fence rows.

Harvey was reported as having said to his wife, Florence, as they rocked in their swing on their front porch the third Sunday night in August, "I believe the Holy Spirit did come to Burr's Branch again this year!"[1]

This story shows how some churches work with annual events or projects. So, instead of buying a denominational calendar and trying to do the kind of detailed annual planning I spoke of earlier, try the event/project kind of planning.

Just go down to the local feed store. Pick up one of their calendars. "Mark off" the second week in August for revival. Include on the calendar the usual date for Vacation Bible School, homecoming, the sweetheart banquet, and the Easter sunrise service. Because many single-staff churches feel good about these events, the wise pastor will affirm these events.

As pastor, don't step in and take over. Instead, become involved in these annual events or projects. Find out who the leaders are for these events. Then, demonstrate to the congregation your willingness to be a good follower. After five to seven years (the time usually required in a family-chapel church for the "preacher" to make an impact on the church's administration), the church will have so accepted you into their trust that they will also be ready to accept your leadership in some areas. You can move toward an intentional approach to annual planning and programming only when the church gives you that right.

Besides, did you know these annual "events and projects" can become the basis for the kind of programmatic planning you would like the church to do later? Here's how.

Consider how these events and projects can support the functions of the church (worship, minister, proclaim and witness, nurture and educate). Find out what resources are needed for these events. Discover how the leaders of these events plan and promote them. As you pull together this information, lead the church to develop a formal process for planning each of these annual events. You then will have the beginnings of an initial, annual calendar.

An additional approach is to use the sentiment and warm feeling attached to these annual events. For example, you might use the homecoming event to initiate some long-range planning for the maintenance and improvement of the church building and cemetery (if there is one). For years, it probably has been part of the congregation's goal to have made some significant improvements on the building in time for homecoming.

Another idea is to attach a seasonal visitation program to the annual revival. While you might not have a regular, ongoing visitation (because "everybody knows everybody" or "they know we have a church down here"), your people might be willing to visit for the revival.

While affirming and supporting these annual events and projects, you will be using their strengths as a way of addressing important needs in the life of the church and maybe paving the way for the day when you move the church toward intentional, program planning.

These kinds of ideas will enable you to accommodate to the rhythm of the congregation rather than trying to get them to accommodate to "big time" planning.

What Type of Guide
I have been reading regularly one church's weekly newsletter. The pastor of this church has been wanting for quite some time to lead the church into a meaningful planning process. For several weeks the pastor wrote persuasive articles about the importance of planning, goal setting, and developing a mission statement. After several weeks of these kinds of articles, a survey was given to the congregation. Church members were asked to complete the survey which dealt with the church's future direction.

A few weeks later, I read this paragraph in the pastor's column of the newsletter: "The most written comment from the survey concerned Church Training. Without a staff minister trained in religious education, it is difficult for our members to receive quality training or to have a Church Training program for all ages. Our state convention sponsors workshops for Church Training workers, but our members would often have to drive long distances to these meetings."

I read those words with a note of sadness. I had certain assumptions. This pastor was more concerned about adding another staff member than he was that the church develop a sense of direction. This pastor did not know how to develop a core of leaders in his church. He wasn't willing to spend time equipping his people. This pastor had his own private agenda. This pastor was unaware of the fine training opportunities provided by the association, state, the Baptist Sunday School Board, or at Ridgecrest and Glorieta Baptist Conference Centers.

I am convinced that if a pastor is to help a church grow, he must commit himself to that church. He will listen to the people and search for ways to help them get where they feel they need to go. The pastor, as a guide, responds to the challenge. He helps the church overcome roadblocks rather than erecting roadblocks in front of the people.

What follows are seven proven guidelines for the leader to use in guiding the church toward balanced, biblical growth. Develop and personally direct the strategy for growth. Here's how:

1. Make the biblical truths of witnessing and outreach central in preaching and teaching.

2. Conduct worship services that are warm and challenging and that create expectancy and hope.

3. Build a fellowship climate that is warm and expresses a witnessing-outreach concern for all persons.

4. Equip and motivate laypersons to be involved in the strategy your church has developed for growth.

5. Use the Sunday School as the growth-outreach arm of the church.

6. Train all believers to know and become involved in the growth cycles of witnessing to others.

7. Establish new fellowships of believers in all cultural settings.[2]

As a church leader, pray for the vision, guidance, and the power of the Holy Spirit to help your church become what it should be. Cultivate, equip, and challenge the church's leadership team to accept biblical, balanced church growth as a priority concern. Then, celebrate the work of the Holy Spirit and the victories the church achieves. Use the enthusiasm and energy of victory to lead the church to set new goals. As each sunset approaches, the pastor begins preparing the people for the next sunrise!

Remember this story? An Englishman was cutting through some underbrush. Exhausted from swinging his machete, he asked the African guide," How far is it to the trail?" The guide responded, "B'wana, we are the trail!"

[1]Taken from the July 1988 issue of *Church Administration,* 17.
[2]See Bruce Grubbs, author-compiler, *Helping a Small Church Grow* (Nashville: Convention Press, 1980), 94.

Resources

Brown, J. Truman, Jr. *Church Planning a Year at a Time.* Nashville: Convention Press, 1984.

Brown, J. Truman, Jr. *How to Conduct a Spiritual Directions Emphasis: Retreat and Annual Planning Guide.* Nashville: Convention Press, 1985.

Brown, J. Truman, Jr. *Planning for the Next Five Years in a Southern Baptist Church.* Nashville: Convention Press, 1989.

Church Administration, May issue, Church Literature Dated Form.

Church Evaluation Survey, Undated Materials Order Form.

Church Members Resource Unit: Church Long-Range Planning. Undated Materials Order Form.

Dale, Robert D. *To Dream Again.* Nashville: Broadman Press, 1981.

McDonough, Reginald M. *Leading Your Church in Long-Range Planning.* Nashville: Convention Press, 1975.

The Church Study
——— Course ———

The Church Study Course is a Southern Baptist education system consisting of short courses for adults and youth. It is complete with recognition, records, and reports. More than 500 courses are available in 23 subject areas.

How to Request Credit for this Course

This book is the text for course number 23044 in the subject area "Pastoral Ministries." Credit for this course may be obtained by reading the book and completing the form on the following page. Mail this form to the Awards Office, Sunday School Board, 127 Ninth Avenue, North, Nashville, Tennessee 37234. A record of your awards will be maintained by the Awards Office.

CHURCH STUDY COURSE
ENROLLMENT/CREDIT REQUEST (FORM-725)

PERSONAL CSC NUMBER (If Known)

INSTRUCTIONS:
1. Please PRINT or TYPE.
2. COURSE CREDIT REQUEST—Requirements must be met. Use exact title.
3. ENROLLMENT IN DIPLOMA PLANS—Enter selected diploma title to enroll.
4. For additional information see the Church Study Course Catalog.
5. Duplicate additional forms as needed. Free forms are available from the Awards Office and State Conventions.

TYPE OF REQUEST: (Check all that apply)
- ☐ Course Credit
- ☐ Enrollment in Diploma Plan
- ☐ Address Change
- ☐ Name Change
- ☐ Church Change

REQUEST FOR

	DATE OF BIRTH		
	Month	Day	Year

☐ Mr. ☐ Miss
☐ Mrs.

Name (First, MI, Last)

Street, Route, or P.O. Box

City, State, Zip Code

CHURCH

Church Name

Mailing Address

City, State, Zip Code

COURSE CREDIT REQUEST

Course No. 23044	Use exact title 1. Guiding the Single-Staff Church
Course No.	Use exact title 2.
Course No.	Use exact title 3.
Course No.	Use exact title 4.
Course No.	Use exact title 5.

ENROLLMENT IN DIPLOMA PLANS

If you have not previously indicated a diploma(s) you wish to earn, or you are beginning work on a new one(s), select and enter the diploma title from the current Church Study Course Catalog. Select one that relates to your leadership responsibility or interest. When all requirements have been met, the diploma will be automatically mailed to your church. No charge will be made for enrollment or diplomas.

Title of diploma	Age group or area
1.	
Title of diploma	Age group or area
2.	

Signature of Pastor, Teacher, or Study Leader	Date

MAIL THIS REQUEST TO
CHURCH STUDY COURSE AWARDS OFFICE
RESEARCH SERVICES DEPARTMENT
127 NINTH AVENUE, NORTH
NASHVILLE, TENNESSEE 37234

FORM-725 (Rev. 7-83)

DATE DUE

AG 4 '92			
FE 7'94			
MR 9'94			
MR30'95			
AP28'95			